DEVELOPING YOUTH LEADERSHIP
THROUGH SPORT

Developing Youth Leadership through Sport

MARK MUNGAL

COPYRIGHT © 2018 MARK MUNGAL
All rights reserved.

DEVELOPING YOUTH LEADERSHIP THROUGH SPORT

ISBN 978-1-5445-1050-7 *Paperback*
      978-1-5445-1049-1 *Ebook*

To the dedicated coaches, teachers, and community volunteers who add amazing value to the lives of young people through the powerful medium of sport.

Contents

FOREWORD 9
INTRODUCTION 11

SECTION ONE: OVERARCHING PRINCIPLES OF TEACHING LEADERSHIP

1. AWAKENING KNOWLEDGE 33
2. DESIGNING LEARNING EXPERIENCES 47
3. REFLECTING 71
4. THE FACILITATOR'S ROLE 85

SECTION TWO: DEVELOPING LEADERSHIP SKILLS

5. COMMUNICATION 113
6. TEAMWORK 133
7. RESOURCEFULNESS 143
8. ADAPTABILITY 157
9. DELEGATION 169
10. DECISION MAKING 183
11. INITIATIVE 203
12. GETTING THINGS DONE 213

CONCLUSION 231
ACKNOWLEDGMENTS 237
ABOUT THE AUTHOR 239

Foreword

BY ANDRE COLLINS

In my teaching experience at the University of Trinidad and Tobago, a question that often incited deep and passionate debate was, "Are leaders born or made?" It was generally agreed that although some people may seem to have a greater propensity to lead, whether you're the head coach of a community football team or the CEO of a successful business, effective leadership is a skillful art that can be developed through careful and deliberate commitment.

I first met Mark Mungal at Teachers' Training College while I was a student and Mark, a physical education lecturer. Even though my elective was psychology and not physical education, we soon became fast friends, as his philosophy of education and sport was very much aligned to my own. Mark's energy was infectious, and if you've met him, you know what I mean. Mark also has an amazing ability to link pedagogical principles to practical applications in meaningful ways.

Our relationship grew into a business partnership with the establishment of the Trinidad and Tobago Alliance for Sports & Physical Education (TTASPE), now the Caribbean Sport and Development Agency (CSDA). In that time, we were able to explore and develop many of the ideas he shares in this book. In the next few pages, you will find some real gems that will make your efforts easier while working with young people. They are tested ideas built on sound philosophical and theoretical principles. Anyone reading this book will be tapping into more than three decades of experience from an industry thinker, an educator, an administrator, a mentor, and a *leader*.

Introduction

People often say things such as "Let's play basketball after school," or "My team is playing volleyball this weekend." But in a sense, people aren't just *playing* sport; they're engaged in something real! When we step onto the field or court—whether it's a neighborhood pickup game or a professional championship—we're involved in an authentic experience filled with real emotion and real interpersonal interactions.

These core interrelated aspects of sport—*authenticity, emotion, relationships*—make it a powerful medium for developing youth leadership skills (figure I.1).

THE POWER OF SPORT

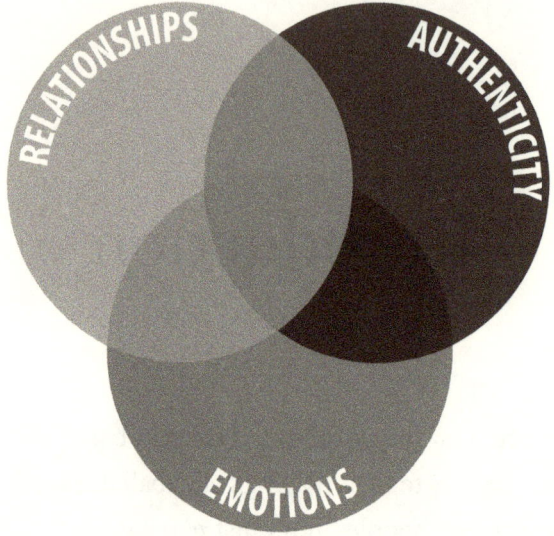

Figure I.1: The Power of Sport

THE POWER OF SPORT

AUTHENTICITY

Fifteen years ago, my colleagues and I started a non-profit organization now called the Caribbean Sport and Development Agency (CSDA). A core part of our work involves facilitating workshops and delivering presentations throughout the Caribbean to enhance the capacity of physical education teachers and coaches who use sport as a tool for youth development. Many of the concepts, principles, and methods shared in this book come from these CSDA adventures.

At one such workshop, the attendees had been sitting in a conference room for a while listening to presentations from various experts. Recognizing that energy levels were dropping, when it was time for our presentation, we decided to ditch the PowerPoint and switch to a hands-on throw-and-catch game. We asked the participants to crumple up paper into balls, and we shifted the furniture out of the way to create an open "playing" space. By the time we divided the participants into teams, the atmosphere had already changed. It was no longer just an activity at a workshop. Participants almost immediately became more relaxed and casual in their interactions. Their overall body language transformed from the conference-room posturing to the playground swagger. Speaking tones shifted from formal and inhibited to friendly and outgoing. The crumpled paper was now a real ball, and the participants were now actively engaged in a real sport experience that brought out a different energy level and a familiarity among the participants that is not common to other settings—that's the authentic nature of sport.

This authenticity is one of the core characteristics of sport that makes it so powerful, and as with many powerful things, if we harness that power, we can achieve great results. At the same time, if we don't manage that power effectively, it can as easily lead to undesirable outcomes. The reality is that the **power of sport can be good, bad, or ugly.** The positive outcomes include strong and meaningful relationships, discipline, focus, team building, skill development, physical fitness, and many others. However, the sport environment can also encourage some less favorable results, such as cheating, discrimination, substance abuse, and violence (including child abuse).

The good, bad, and ugly outcomes appear at every level of sport because every level facilitates authentic engagement, whether it's a backyard game of volleyball or World Cup football in Brazil.[1] Part of our responsibility as coaches and physical education teachers is to harness the power of sport to facilitate the generation of positive outcomes in youth. Children and young people don't automatically become focused, cooperative, and disciplined because they play sports. But they can, if we know how to use sport to generate positive, meaningful results. We also have a responsibility to safeguard children and young people from the negative effects associated with poor practice in sport.

EMOTIONS

Sport is also powerful because it generates real emotions. At every skill level, participants experience a wide range of emotions, including authentic joy and sorrow, excitement and frustration, pain and pleasure.

---

[1] Throughout the book, the word *football* refers to the sport known as soccer in the United States.

In 2005, Trinidad and Tobago's senior men's football team played Bahrain in a World Cup qualifying match. The Trinidad and Tobago team included several multimillionaire players—professionals who played at the highest level in the United Kingdom, Europe, and the United States. These were footballers who, over the course of their careers, had won major professional titles for their respective clubs.

In the dying minutes of the game against Bahrain, Trinidad and Tobago scored a header to win the match and secure a spot in the World Cup. When the final whistle blew, these big men, who had been playing at the highest level all their lives, were in tears—not just crying but embracing each other and sobbing uncontrollably for the entire world to see. This single game of football caused them to experience real, intense emotions—that's the power of sport.

These emotions are not limited to elite sport; they can be experienced during informal participation settings as well. If someone makes a three-pointer in a pickup game of basketball, he or she may feel genuine satisfaction, joy, and excitement. Similarly, if two players on a team don't pass the ball to a third person, that left-out teammate may feel real frustration. Players experience the full range of emotions at all levels in sport: anger, ecstasy, sadness, happiness, and misery. Our role as coaches and physical education teachers is not so much to control the emotional experiences of young people but to create youth-friendly sport environments that allow participants to express their emotions, and then to harness that emotional power to teach life lessons.

RELATIONSHIPS

In an authentic sport setting, we interact with one another in unique ways. For example, consider the physical contact that's acceptable in sport but not in everyday interactions. At the workshop mentioned earlier, participants sat at tables, listened to the speaker, and talked to one another, but they didn't high-five or jump into each other's arms. However, as soon as we created a game (albeit with paper balls), the level of acceptable physical contact changed. All of a sudden, it was OK to celebrate with hugs and butt slaps.

When we are actively engaged in a sport experience, our responses to situations tend to differ from other settings. In the sport setting, we often drop our guard and become vulnerable. We become so involved in the game—the missed catch, the bad call, a goal scored—that we react naturally and spontaneously, and by doing so, we show others who we really are. We can't help it; that's the power of sport.

In that real setting, we are no longer doctors, lawyers,

teachers, or postal workers; we are all on the same team, wearing the same uniform, focused on the same goal. Sport brings people together from all walks of life, from different ethnicities, religions, and socioeconomic classes. When we're on the field, there's no hierarchy based on wealth or any other classification; sport creates a level playing field.

The relationships formed through sport are often strong and long-lasting. Here's a personal example: I have played football with the same group of friends for more than thirty years. We play against a different team every weekend, and midweek, we play a short-sided "small-goal sweat" at our high school. Because of years of playing football together, we have come to know, understand, and value one another's strengths and weaknesses, flaws and vulnerabilities, and even though we all differ in many ways, we've developed a strong sense of camaraderie and solidarity that transcends traditional friendships. These are not superficial relationships; they are based on years of playing sport together that have led to teamwork in other dimensions of our lives—joint adventures recreationally, socially, professionally, and through several charitable endeavors. That's the power of sport—the power to create lifelong friendships.

The people who attend the CSDA training workshops are usually coaches, physical education teachers, sport administrators, and volunteers who work with children and young people in a sport setting. In our workshops, rather than share information in declarative presentations, we use a more indirect approach and include a lot of interactive activities that bring out the concepts and principles that the participants will then use with their students and players.

In one of our coaching education workshops, we use a role-reversal strategy to bring out key concepts. We put coaches into teams for the five days of the workshop, and during parts of the workshop, the coaches role-play as children, while the workshop facilitators play the role of coaches. Even though the participants are role-playing (as children), as soon as they begin to participate in game situations, they become immersed in the authentic sport setting, which often leads to the same emotions that we discussed earlier: some have lots of fun, others get frustrated, and at least one or two become angry.

This happens almost every time we have coaches take on the role of the player: They become so involved in the game, almost as if they're in a different world, and they let down their guard, often reacting spontaneously and naturally. Sometimes that means shouting at a colleague in the heat of the moment, and if the reaction is not managed, it can lead to arguments. Sometimes, as facilitators we deliberately trigger these emotions as it allows us to debrief and share conflict resolution tools coaches can use with their players to prevent and resolve conflict. Of course, we could simply share all of this information in a PowerPoint presentation, but letting the coaches experience these situations in an authentic sport setting has far greater impact.

WHAT IS LEADERSHIP?

If you Google "leadership," you will find several definitions, many of them conflicting. In this book, we define leadership as *a set of skills that someone uses to achieve an intended goal*. In this sense, leadership doesn't involve having a certain personality; it's a skill set that anyone can learn and use—not just the designated leader of a team, organization, or community.

A football team, for example, has eleven players on the field, and each player has a different role. The midfielder is the playmaker. The striker scores goals. The defender keeps opponents away from the goal.

Captain is another role; this person keeps the team united and focused. The captain may be the team leader, but he or she isn't the only player who demonstrates leadership skills. The goalkeeper, for example, tells the defenders where to stand on a free kick. The utility player decides when to drop back to help the defenders. Each player uses leadership skills within the context of his or her specific role.

The good news is that **leadership skills can be learned.** In the same way that children and young people can learn math, reading, and writing skills, they can also learn leadership skills. Likewise, leadership skills can be practiced, improved, and then applied in everyday situations: in the home, at school, in social settings, and beyond. Because sport is authentic, emotional, and interactive, it's a very powerful medium for facilitating leadership skills development—not the only medium but one we have found to be very effective.

SPORT PROVIDES AUTHENTIC OPPORTUNITIES TO LEAD

Leadership in youth sport is sometimes treated as a status symbol rather than a tool to facilitate development.[2] For example, some coaches pick a captain—often the star player—to call the coin toss or shake hands at midfield. Although these roles are usually assigned to the team leader, they do not require any meaningful leadership capacity—but they may help a young person feel valued. There's nothing wrong with awarding the title of captain

---

2 Daniel Gould and Dana K. Voelker, "Youth Sport Leadership Development: Leveraging the Sports Captaincy Experience," *Journal of Sport Psychology in Action* 1, no. 1 (2010): 1-14, https://doi.org/10.1080/21520704.2010.497695.

based on ability or seniority, and there's certainly nothing wrong with assigning symbolic roles to team leaders, but that's not the focus of this book.

Instead, we give suggestions for using sport roles such as captain to facilitate leadership skills development. Our model proposes that every youth sport participant be given the opportunity to take on a leadership role—for example, captain, coach, team manager, referee, sport journalist, and so on—that would provide authentic opportunities to learn and apply leadership skills.

Sport provides many opportunities to develop and practice leadership skills, both on and off the field. In this book, we'll highlight some authentic situations that enable young people to hone their leadership skills in school and community sport settings.

LEADERSHIP INVOLVES POWER

In many youth leadership programs, adults hold the power. For example, the teachers who support after-school clubs might let students elect a president, but the teachers still decide on the group's direction, how they're going to get there, and so on. This book suggests a different approach: help students exercise leadership skills by letting them make decisions.

It's not easy for us, the adult coaches and teachers, to transfer that decision-making power. At CSDA workshops, we show adults not only how to give up that power but also how to give youth the tools to make good choices. Leadership involves making decisions based on the smartest, most socially responsible choice in a given situation.

Young people (people!) often make decisions based on peer pressure. We want to help youth make decisions based on what's best and not on what everyone else is doing. For example, if a young person sees sports equipment has been left out in the sports hall or on the playground, he or she can leave it and go home, because that's what everyone else is doing, or make a socially responsible choice to put it away.

Ultimately, we want youth to recognize they have the power to make a difference in the lives of others, and not just in the sport setting. We use sport to develop leadership skills, but the goal is to transfer that learning to other dimensions of their lives.

LEADERSHIP INVOLVES SERVITUDE

As mentioned, sport is a powerful medium for development, but the outcomes can be good, bad, or ugly. The same is true of leadership. Someone might learn to grab the power inherent in leadership and make poor choices. Consider, for example, gang leaders or drug lords: they use their leadership for unscrupulous and illegal activities.

Our role as coaches and teachers is to help youth use that leadership power for good—for volunteering and serving others, for enhancing their schools and communities, and for making positive contributions to society. We want to develop servant leaders.

TEACHING PERSONAL AND SOCIAL RESPONSIBILITY

Don Hellison worked in the physical education and teacher education field in Chicago, Illinois, in an area where young people were deeply involved in drugs and gang activity. Hellison developed a model called TPSR—Teaching Personal and Social Responsibility—and proposed that physical education can be used to develop more than sport skills and improved health; it can also facilitate the learning of life or social skills such as anger management and conflict resolution.

> In education, there are three learning domains: cognitive (knowledge), psychomotor (physical skills), and affective (attitudes/values/emotions). The CSDA leadership model caters to all three domains, and Hellison's TPSR falls under the affective domain: values such as trust, cooperation, and respect.

In developing our youth leadership model, we have adopted many of Hellison's ideas. For example, Hellison's model starts with self-identification. Likewise, we ask participants to identify where they currently stand with regard to the values being presented (e.g., they ask themselves, "Am I cooperating with others? Am I cooperating all the time or just when told to?") and where they want to be.

We have also adopted Hellison's idea of focusing on a few specific values (referred to as *life skills* in this book) in each youth program. Those life skills vary, depending on the needs of the school or community in which the program is held. If the community is experiencing a lot of violence, for example, the program might focus on conflict resolution. Or we might focus on respect. Then within respect, we might break it down further: respect for self, respect for others, and respect for equipment.

Finally, we present these areas of personal and social responsibility as skills, in the same way that serving a volleyball and shooting a three-pointer are skills. We find the sport setting is a powerful place where participants can learn, practice, and apply these life skills.

WHY EMPHASIZE THESE CONCEPTS?

This book proposes that leadership skills are not just for the outstanding boy or girl who becomes captain; they are for everyone. In the same way that all students need to learn to read and write, they all need to know how to lead. At some stage or context in life, everyone will use these skills—whether in a family, community, sport, or work situation. Everyone will have opportunities to make socially responsible choices that benefit others. Thus, it's important that coaches, physical education teachers, volunteers—anyone who works with youth—know how to facilitate the development of these skills.

It's also important to remember that developing new skills takes time. Even if a young person learns a particular leadership behavior, he or she might not use that skill in an immediately observable way. The goal is to awaken skills that youth can use for a lifetime; coaches and teachers can trust that their intervention has made an impact, even if it's not seen right away.

There are many effective educational platforms for developing strong youth leaders, including music, scouting, and sport programs. We have found sport provides an authentic setting for communicating, awakening, and developing leadership skills. The CSDA Youth Sport Leadership Model is the framework through which we use sport to develop leadership skills.

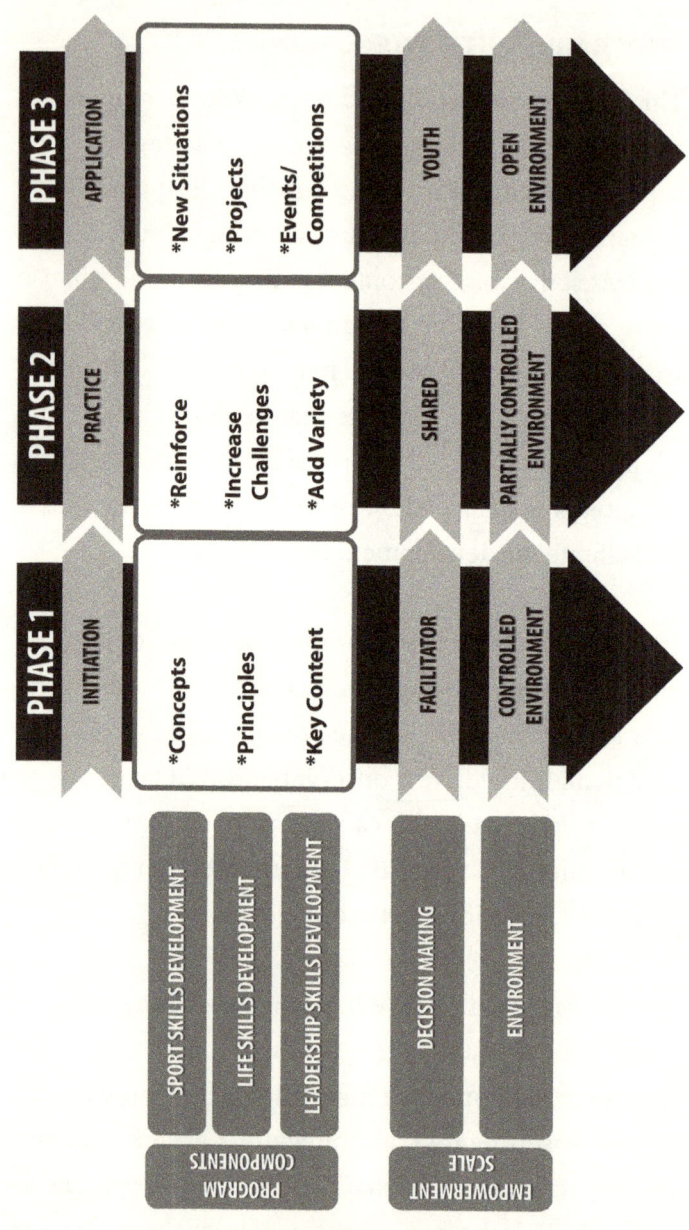

Figure I.2: CSDA Youth Sport Leadership Model

THE CSDA APPROACH TO YOUTH LEADERSHIP DEVELOPMENT

In the 1980s, Daryl Siedentop started developing the Sport Education Model. He wanted to improve students' experience in physical education classes by teaching them sport skills in the context of a real game. At the same time, Siedentop's model gave every student the chance to take on leadership roles in a setting that closely resembled an authentic sport experience.

Although Siedentop wasn't focused on leadership per se, the framework he developed provides the perfect context for introducing and practicing leadership and other life skills. In this framework, participants are divided into teams for a ten- to twelve-week project—for example, planning a basketball tournament. Each person chooses a role that has certain responsibilities in the context of that tournament. For example, the roles to choose from might be coach, referee, journalist, team manager, and first aider. As youth participate in the planning and executing of the tournament, they take on real leadership roles making real decisions in a real sport setting (the process will be described later with examples).

Figure I.2 summarizes the model we propose for developing youth leadership. It's an adaptation of Siedentop's Sport Education Model and focuses on three areas: sport skills, leadership skills, and life skills (the personal and social responsibility values introduced by Hellison). As young people move through the three phases (Initiation, Practice, Application), they develop skills in the three key areas and gain practice in applying those skills.

The CSDA Youth Sport Leadership Model relies heavily on high-quality sport experiences as the platform for skills communication. As young people engage in these authentic sport settings and take on real leadership roles, they develop skills in all three areas. In this book, we focus on leadership skills, but participants also learn sport and life skills in the process.

Three overarching principles guide each phase of leadership development:

1. Awaken knowledge in the participants
2. Facilitate experiences to reinforce and practice that knowledge
3. Encourage reflection on those experiences

Section one of this book discusses each principle in turn, and section two describes eight leadership skills young people learn as these principles are applied in rich sport experiences. The CSDA workshops with coaches and teachers follow these same three principles, as does the presentation of ideas in this book. The goal is to awaken knowledge in you, the facilitator; to give examples of how rich experiences can be facilitated; and to offer questions for reflection.

A REAL-LIFE EXAMPLE

In early 2017, my brothers and I went camping with about fifty secondary school boys, ages eleven to sixteen. We took them to a campsite at Scotland Bay, one of several beautiful spots off the northwestern peninsula of Trinidad.

On the last day of the camp, there was an incident between two boys—Austin, who was fourteen, and Greg, who was sixteen and had stepped up as a leader among the group. A situation arose because Austin kept crossing the line—messing around with other boys' clothes and other unacceptable behavior.

For the most part, the boys handle these situations on their own, so Greg took it upon himself to talk to Austin about his behavior. Unfortunately, their conversation deteriorated into physical contact with both boys losing their tempers. I was out swimming at the time, and when I returned, the other boys briefed me on what had happened. I let some time pass, and then I discreetly pulled Greg and Austin aside for a private conversation.

Instead of telling them what they should have done, I invited them to talk to each other about the situation while

I stood by and listened. Without any prompting, Greg started by saying, "Austin, I apologize. This is my fault. I handled this badly. Look, there are some things that you were doing that we needed to talk about, but when I came to talk about it, you showed me attitude and then I responded poorly. I should not have responded the way that I did, but we need to talk about those things."

Greg went on to tell Austin how he thought Austin was going to be a good leader someday. This moment was so powerful that the tough fourteen-year-old was almost in tears. At that point, I moved away and allowed them to continue their conversation. The young men discussed and resolved the matter in a very mature manner without any significant input from me.

This situation illustrates what we hope to achieve with the CSDA model: give young people opportunities to lead, reflect, and devise their own solutions. The more we do that—the more we give them rich, meaningful opportunities to lead—the more they will take those steps to become true servant leaders.

# SECTION ONE

Overarching Principles of Teaching Leadership

CHAPTER 1

Awakening Knowledge

When I was about eight years old, I read a poem in *Nelson's West Indian Reader*. The verses remained somewhere in my subconscious until about eight years ago when one particular line came back to me:

> HE WHO KNOWS AND KNOWS NOT HE
> KNOWS IS ASLEEP—WAKE HIM.

This line captures the theory of change behind the CSDA leadership model and programs: Young people already know everything they need to know. We don't need to tell them what it means to lead; our responsibility as teachers and coaches is to awaken the knowledge they already possess.

As seen in the story about Greg, I didn't have to tell him anything in that situation. He knew what he had to do to make things right with Austin. Of course, Greg benefited from his experiences growing up under this leadership model, but at that moment, in that tense situation, he knew how to demonstrate leadership without an adult giving him direction.

As mentioned earlier, sport is a powerful medium that can potentially lead to bad and sometimes ugly outcomes, in addition to the many beneficial ones. Similarly, the knowledge young people already have is both positive and negative; while they know how to make decisions and communicate, for example, they also have the capacity to lie and steal. Our responsibility is to facilitate the awakening of knowledge that leads to positive results that benefit others.

The development of youth leaders is facilitated through authentic learning experiences designed to awaken the knowledge, skills, and values that are essential for effective leadership.

THE AWAKENING PROCESS

There are four steps in facilitating the awakening of knowledge. These steps are repeated in each phase of the CSDA Youth Sport Leadership Model, but especially in phase 1,

Initiation, where we design experiences and introduce skills for the first time.

1. DESIGN

As facilitators, we design learning experiences based on what we want the young people to learn. Thus, we must first decide which specific skill or skills we want to awaken.

In the CSDA model, we focus on three potential areas: leadership skills (e.g., communication, decision making), sport skills (e.g., passing to targets, shooting three-pointers), and life skills (e.g., respect, anger management). In this book, we're focusing on leadership skills, but because of the authentic nature of sport, life skills and sport skills are developed as well.

The focus of youth sport leadership programs varies from group to group. We choose skills and design learning experiences based on the needs of the participants, issues in the community, and other factors. Volunteers and coaches in the community can provide feedback to help you decide what skills to work on and what learning experiences will be most effective. One important guideline: the focus skill should fit the group; it should not be forced.

2. ENGAGE

The goal of the carefully designed learning experience is to engage young people in an activity that challenges them. Whether we seek to improve serving accuracy (sports) or to develop delegation skills (leadership), we want participants physically, mentally, and emotionally involved in the task at hand. If the experience is too easy or too difficult, it won't engage young people and it won't lead to desired results. Similarly, if it does not create interest or excitement, young people will be disengaged.

3. CHALLENGE

To challenge the young people and keep them engaged, we may need to manipulate or modify the environment. Throughout the learning experience, our responsibility as facilitators is to observe, assess, and make changes to ensure the experience is meaningful and relevant; in other words, we need to make sure the experience is awakening the intended knowledge and make changes if it's not. This is called the *diagnostic-prescriptive approach* and will be discussed more in chapter 4. We might need to change a rule, add a task, or remove an obstacle to keep it appropriately challenging and to achieve the intended goal.

4. REFLECT

Reflection is a key part of the awakening process. To

make sure young people are grasping the intended skills, we debrief and encourage them to think about what they did during the challenge. Although we list reflection as the fourth step, it takes place throughout the learning experience. Awakening of knowledge happens during reflection.

SAMPLE LEARNING EXPERIENCES TO AWAKEN KNOWLEDGE

If you Google "icebreaker," you will probably find many fun games that can be used as learning experiences. The key is to connect the icebreaker to a lesson so the activity has value. Here are a few examples of learning experiences designed to awaken different skills.

ZIP, ZAP, BOING

In our youth programs, we use an icebreaker called Zip, Zap, Boing. Small groups stand in a circle facing inward and use the words *zip*, *zap*, *boing* to represent different gestures: pointing to the left is a *zip*, pointing to the right is a *zap*, and pointing across the circle is a *boing*. Players have to react quickly to changes in direction and remember what each word/gesture means.

Zip, Zap, Boing makes people laugh because they forget what the words mean and what gestures they should be making, but the game can also be an effective learning experience with a little modification.

We often use Zip, Zap, Boing to focus on communication and/or peer education. For example, we might divide the large group into smaller teams and have one person from each team join the organizer at the front of the room. The organizer hands each person a sheet of instructions and says, "We're going to play Zip, Zap, Boing. Here are the directions. Read them over, and then teach your team how to play. Then we'll have a competition." One person on each team now has the opportunity to practice leadership skills; it's their responsibility to teach their team how to be good Zip, Zap, Boingers.

Following the activity, we debrief and discuss the team experience based on the particular skill that we focused on (e.g., communication). So instead of telling the young people how to communicate the Zip, Zap, Boing rules to their teammates, we simply give them the instructions, let them execute the task, and then afterward have a discussion. We may ask, "How did your coach communicate the instructions to the team? What was effective? What could have been done to improve the communication?" Without being told, young people already know the key guidelines for good communication. This learning experience simply facilitates the awakening of that knowledge.

POINT OF CONTACT

Rather than tell young people about grip and stance and back lifts and point of contact and follow-through, we can create learning experiences that help them understand these sport skills. For example, in one of our volleyball drills, participants serve the ball at targets. Where the ball goes partly depends on the point of contact—where the hand meets the ball. If the player hits the ball on its underside, for example, it goes up. We tell the young people to explore hitting the ball in different ways, let them engage in the experience, and then debrief. We might ask, "How did you contact the ball? Which point of contact was most successful? Why was it most successful?"

Without any prompting from the facilitators, participants can tell us that if they hit with an open hand, they have more control; with a closed hand, they get a little more power but they lose control. Players can tell us this because they experienced it. They were challenged to hit accurately and experimented hitting with a closed fist, open fist, forearm, and so on; they tried hitting while their feet were close together and while they were straddled. Then they had an opportunity to analyze what happened, and they figured out what worked and what didn't.

WRITING RULES TO A GAME

This example can be used to focus on a life skill such

as compromise. We give the participants a few guidelines—for example, they have a certain amount of space and specific equipment and a predetermined amount of time—and have them come up with rules for a game to be played under those conditions.

First, the participants work alone and come up with their own game and rules. Then we pair them off. After each person shares, the pairs agree on one set of rules. Then that pair joins another pair, and they discuss their games and come to an agreement. Then a representative from each group of four comes together, and they determine the final set of rules.

We have used a version of this experience with adults in a sport administration workshop. A significant part of sport administration revolves around managing conflict, which is a life skill or value. We have participants design a new game, and we give them limitations based on the materials and space we have available. The adults come up with hilarious games, but the most important part is the learning experience: working with other people and coming to an agreement. In these situations, some people insist on their own ideas, and this gives us an opportunity to debrief and reflect on concepts such as compromise and conflict resolution. At the end of the workshop, we always play the new game.

Another version of the rules challenge involves giving young people the opportunity to write the rules for a basketball tournament. The tournament follows the basic rules of basketball, and the participants make modifications to certain aspects: number of players on a team, length of each period, number of substitutions per game, and so on. We might impose constraints, but the young people do all the rule making.

Afterward, we ask questions to help the young people reflect and debrief. For example, "I noticed you did this. Why?" They might explain, for example, that because there is no fencing around the court, when the ball goes out of bounds, retrieving it takes a while. They decided to throw in another ball to avoid wasting time.

In these learning experiences, there's an element of accountability and an element of critical reviewing. That's what true leadership involves. Participants are given a real task that produces real results; they learn that they can bring real value to the situation. As they apply these newly awakened skills (phase 3 of the CSDA model), youth experience more success and more productivity.

GUIDELINES FOR FACILITATORS

Here are some tips to keep in mind as you focus on the process of awakening knowledge.

1. YOUNG PEOPLE HAVE CAPACITY

As educators, we need to remember that young people already have knowledge, and we need to treat them as if they do. Many educators talk about the importance of youth leadership, but they still tell young people, "This is what leadership is about." They give young people everything instead of letting them figure it out.

If you have a group of young people brainstorm the elements of leadership, they will come up with key points. Given this task, youth often mention the ability to influence people. If you press them and ask, "What do you mean? How does that work?" they can clearly flesh out that idea. Young people have capacity to think at this level.

2. EVERY YOUNG PERSON HAS VALUE

Our responsibility as adults is to help young people recognize their own value. Some don't realize their self-worth because they're repeatedly told, "You're young. You don't matter." We don't give young people value, but we help them recognize the value they already have. We do this by giving them authentic tasks that have meaning. So, for example, rather than making someone team captain in name only, you might say, "Tim, I need you to organize the equipment bin and make a schedule of who will take it to practice each day." This gives the individual a meaningful task that involves decision making and leads to real consequences—an organized equipment bin and a schedule that people actually follow.

3. FACILITATING AWAKENING REQUIRES INTUITION

Some young people wake up right away when confronted with a challenge; they immediately grasp the skill or concept. Others hit snooze when the alarm clock goes off. As you build relationships with your players, you will come to understand which ones hit snooze and need a little more prodding.

When I was doing my coaching education in a volleyball setting, I had one instructor who used to say, "You have to smell the air." His point was that we need to be intuitive about what our players need at any given moment, and we can only do that if we really know them. We need to learn when our players are stuck and what it will take to get them unstuck.

As facilitators, we have a responsibility to our players. It's a commitment to each individual. Although we have a lesson that moves from point A to point B, sometimes we need to stop to offer a little help—to "poke" individuals with a shoulder tap or question or eye contact to awaken them. We're not pushing them or forcing them; we're awakening them. The only way to intuitively know what each player needs is to have a relationship with them.

4. YOUNG PEOPLE SHOULD BE TREATED AS INDIVIDUALS

To awaken knowledge in every young person, we need to use different tactics. Even though young people have many similarities, they have different personalities and should be treated as unique individuals.

At our youth leadership camps, for example, we usually have one or two participants who get homesick because it is their first camp experience. We have to know how to treat them to keep them engaged. We also have a few who complain about the smallest things. We don't want them to feel like we're not taking them seriously, but we do want them to develop some toughness. We need to know which tactics will work with each individual to achieve this awakening.

At one camp, a young boy was in tears the first evening because he felt picked on. During the week, he came to me about every little thing. At the end of camp, however, he told me what he had learned: "I became smart." I asked what he meant. He replied, "I learned to defend my snacks." Early in the week, the other guys were stealing his snacks. The young boy formed strategies and felt good about his accomplishment. We need to let youth grow and learn at their own pace based on their own reality.

5. SHARING FACILITATES FURTHER AWAKENING

The reflective process in the learning experiences we create should include a sharing element—a time when young people can share their understandings, thoughts, and observations with their peers. When young people have the opportunity to share their insights in a safe environment, they strengthen their own understandings, but more significantly, others in the group gain further awakening as they listen: they build on each other's ideas and answer questions that may arise, leading to new ideas, better solutions, further clarity, and sometimes more questions that lead to even further exploration and analysis. Part of our role is to facilitate this peer sharing and awakening—in pairs, in small groups, and even in whole-group discussions.

KEY TAKEAWAYS

1. Youth already have a wealth of knowledge related to leadership skills, life skills, and sport skills.

2. The facilitator's role is to awaken that knowledge through carefully designed learning experiences.

3. The facilitator's role is also to help youth share that awakened knowledge with others.

CHAPTER 2

Designing Learning Experiences

There is a difference between learning *about* something and actually learning something. Someone might learn about leadership by reading several leadership books, but that's not the same as learning to lead. Someone might learn about swimming by watching other swimmers, but to actually learn to swim, one must jump in the pool. Likewise, for learning experiences to awaken knowledge, they must facilitate actual learning—not just learning about.

People learn in different ways. Some people like being given information in a straightforward, declarative way; other people learn best by engaging in a hands-on process. The approach being presented here is not the only way to learn, but it works in our leadership model.

ACTIVITY VERSUS LEARNING EXPERIENCE

Let's say a football team comes out to practice. The coach leads a warm-up drill, and then the players kick the ball back and forth in pairs—first short passes and then long ones. The team finishes with a short-sided game; then they gather their things and go home with no further input from the coach. This team has participated in a series of football-related activities; these activities may be fun and get players moving, but they could be more valuable if the coach approached practice a little differently.

Let's say another team comes out to practice. This time, the coach has a few specific goals in mind: she wants players to work on planting their nonkicking foot and turning effectively once they receive a pass. The coach sets up a drill that emphasizes these two skills. After the drill, the coach encourages players to reflect; for example, she asks them to give their thoughts on the best place to plant their foot. After this discussion, the group plays a game in which they focus on practicing the skills they just worked on and discussed. Afterward, the coach debriefs with her players on what happened during the game, and then the players go home.

The first team engaged in a series of activities; the second team engaged in a learning experience. The key difference is that the second coach had a goal—she wanted her team to learn certain sport skills—and she took steps to facilitate this learning.

The same overriding principle applies to the development of life skills and leadership skills: to facilitate learning through sport, we must engage young people in a learning experience that has a clear purpose or desired outcome—we cannot just play a game or activity. As facilitators, we must know up front what life skills or leadership skills we want to awaken and then design the experience accordingly.

Another difference between an activity and a learning experience: once an activity starts, a coach may stand on the sidelines and let the players kick the ball or play the game—unless there's a fight or a need for officiating. With a learning experience, on the other hand, the coach stays fully engaged. He monitors the action to make sure players are appropriately and meaningfully engaged in the learning experience. Sometimes this involves modifying a challenge to bring out a certain reaction and offering solutions to challenges as they arise.

For example, if we want to focus on a life skill such as anger management, we have to deliberately design a learning experience to awaken knowledge and skills for managing anger. Such a learning experience may involve creating (controlled) situations to trigger anger (e.g., making unfair calls against a team or player in a game situation). Then we provide the young people with a tool to use when they become angry: we often use the time-out. In the midst of the experience, the young person discovers what makes him angry: bad calls by the referee. Now he knows the trigger (bad call), and he has a tool (time-out) to use when he feels angry. Depending on the situation, the coach may encourage the team to be involved in the process. They know when their teammate is about to get angry, so they call a team time-out. Eventually, the player wants to get to the point where he recognizes the anger starting and takes a time-out on his own.

LEARNING EXPERIENCES AND THE CSDA MODEL

The learning experience example just described follows the format and phases of the CSDA Youth Sport Leadership Model this book is based on. The model is typically implemented over a regular school term or semester with a group of twenty to thirty young people (usually not fewer than twelve and not more than forty). In the early stages of the program, the young people are placed in equal-ability teams, and each team member chooses a sport-related leadership role (e.g., coach, administrator, official, journalist, first aider, etc.), which they keep for the duration of the program.

Over the course of the school term, participants engage

in various learning experiences that are related to their chosen roles and grounded in the sport setting. These learning experiences involve everything from choosing a team name and logo to creating and playing games to organizing sporting events. The specific skills they learn through these experiences vary, depending on the focus of that particular project, but they always include leadership skills, life skills, and sport skills. The final, culminating event is usually a tournament that participants have planned and organized over the course of the term; the planning and execution of this final sport event give young people a chance to practice and apply the skills they've been learning.

Skill development in the CSDA model takes place in phases. In phase 1 (see figure 2.1), the facilitator controls learning; he doesn't tell the young person the answers, but he does offer carefully guided awakening. In the example given earlier, for instance, the facilitator would know what triggers the player's anger, manipulate the experience to trigger that anger, and then ask the player to take a time-out when anger starts to build. During the time-out, the coach has a task for the player: count backward from ten or sing a happy song; depending on the situation, the coach may even ask the player to come up with his own appropriate time-out plan. It's not punishment; the coach is helping the player awaken anger management skills. Because the skill involves social responsibility, the team may get involved, too. Importantly, during this phase the players begin to understand the *concept* (that anger can be managed) and they become aware of the *principles* involved in anger management (identify the trigger and apply an appropriate tool).

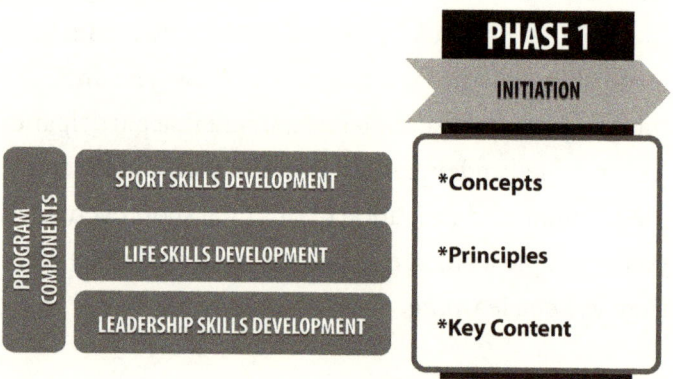

Figure 2.1: *Phase 1 of CSDA Youth Sport Leadership Model*

In phase 2 of the CSDA model (figure 2.2), the facilitator and participant share control of learning. In the anger management example, the coach backs off and lets the player practice with his teammates. The teammates become more aware of the player's triggers; they know that if he gets a bad call from the referee, he will become angry, so they may take a team time-out. The coach may still manipulate the environment by introducing new triggers to generate anger, but unlike phase 1, in this phase, the player or his teammates call the time-out. During phase 2, the coach may intervene to ask questions, encourage reflection, and reinforce positive behaviors.

Sometimes this intervention may occur during a debrief at the end of the session.

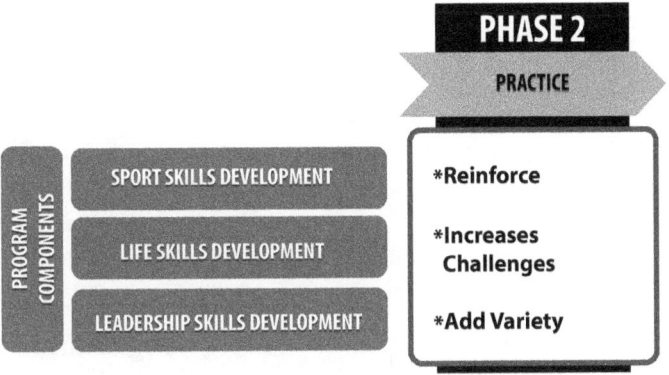

Figure 2.2: Phase 2 of CSDA Youth Sport Leadership Model

In the final phase (figure 2.3), young people apply the concepts and principles awakened in phase 1 and practiced in phase 2. In the earlier example, the young person in phase 3 should be able to control his anger and give himself a time-out if necessary. By this phase, he is now increasingly self-aware, knows what his triggers are, and knows what to do if he gets a bad call. Ideally, the player gets to the point where he doesn't need a time-out; he just counts to ten or sings to himself or breathes deeply for a few seconds. As players move through the phases of leadership skill development, the adult's role decreases.

Figure 2.3: Phase 3 of CSDA Youth Sport Leadership Model

Our responsibility as facilitators is to design learning experiences that allow a person to move through those leadership acquisition phases and gain true learning. Sometimes this means manipulating the experience to increase the challenge. In the preceding anger management life skill lesson, for example, the coach made a bad officiating call in an attempt to trigger anger in her player. The player doesn't know the coach has manipulated the environment. The coach looks at the learning experience and modifies it to create a new challenge for the player.

We could apply the same series of steps if we want to develop leadership skills. For example, after participants are divided into leadership roles, we might create a sport experience to help the youth referees learn to remain calm and assertive under pressure. After the challenging situation, we might debrief with questions and comments such as the following:

- What happened in that game?
- How did you respond?
- What would be a better way to respond?
- What's a key lesson you can learn from this experience?
- You know you should be calm and assertive. How can you remain calm and assertive?
- What are specific things you can do to show that you are calm and assertive?
- How can you use hand gestures to demonstrate that you are being calm?

Whether the intended outcome is passing accuracy (sports skill), anger management (life skill), or learning to be calm and assertive (leadership skill), we need to create a learning experience, not just an activity. It's an engaging process with challenges that allow for reflection. As young people move through the phases, they practice and apply the skills until ultimately, the skills are transferred to other dimensions of their lives: that's the goal.

About ten years ago, we were using the same Youth Sport Leadership Model at a center for young women who had fallen through the cracks of the system. During the day, they attended classes—some academic and some technical/vocational. We were asked to come do a project based on sport and development, so we chose volleyball and trained the staff to help facilitate the project with the girls. We focused on decreasing violence, specifically fights between the girls.

Over the course of the next few months, the girls divided into teams, took on sport-related roles, and started working on anger management in the volleyball setting. The adults provided learning experiences and guidance at first, and then gradually stepped back as the girls moved through the Practice and Application phases. Finally, the girls ran a volleyball tournament on their own.

The staff invited us back to attend the last day of the competition. My colleague Andre and I were the only adults present, because the rest of the staff didn't attend the final day; the girls were completely in charge at this point. Two teams were playing in the game, and the third team was officiating. About halfway through the game, an incident occurred and one of the girls, who was known to be violent, cursed loudly and walked off the court. The team captain approached the official—who was one of her peers—and asked for a time-out. They discussed the situation. The official allowed the team to make a substitution, and the game continued.

During the next set, the girl who had walked off came back and apologized to the referee, who allowed the player back into the game. Play continued with no further problems.

After the game, Andre and I debriefed with the adults. They informed us that under normal circumstances, that situation would have ended in an all-out brawl among the girls. So even though it wasn't perfect—the girl used obscene language and stormed off the court—the event did not have the usual outcome because the girls had started applying anger management skills and they understood the process.

This experience showed us that the model works if you're committed to it. It shows what can happen if adults awaken skills and knowledge in young people—skills and knowledge they already have—and then provide opportunities to practice and apply those skills in real, authentic settings. These girls weren't role-playing. They were playing an actual match and had an actual conflict in which a girl actually got angry; the team took a real time-out and talked to a real referee, who managed the situation. The girls all showed higher-order leadership skills throughout this tense situation that could have otherwise resulted in chaos.

KEY ELEMENTS OF A LEARNING EXPERIENCE
1. SPECIFIC PURPOSE

As mentioned, our first task is to determine the purpose of the learning experience. An activity such as Zip, Zap, Boing, for example, can be turned into several different learning experiences depending on what the purpose is. It can be used to awaken skills in the leadership or life skills domains: communication, feedback, teamwork, respect, and more.

Icebreakers have a lot of potential to develop life skills and leadership skills if we modify them so they focus on a specific skill and involve debriefing and reflecting. Icebreakers are fun, which is great; people engage more in experiences they enjoy. The key is going beyond fun so young people get something out of the activity—a process that generates awakening.

In the CSDA programs, we tend to steer away from the word *teach*. Instead, we use *facilitate* or *awaken*. For us, *teaching* suggests the adults are telling the young people what to do, that the adults know something and the youth don't. As mentioned, young people already possess knowledge; our job is to awaken it.

The learning experience should be designed to produce positive outcomes in one or more of the three educational domains: cognitive (knowledge), psychomotor (skills/techniques), and affective (values). These domains are interactive; awakening happens simultaneously in the different domains. For example, while working on serving or spiking in volleyball (psychomotor), young people may also learn to manage their anger (affective) and show respect (knowledge/leadership) to their teammates. As they think about the technical aspects of sport performance, they also engage emotionally in competition and interact with peers and opponents. If someone is not managing her anger, she is more likely to serve long or wide or into the net because the emotional and technical interact. Likewise, when a player makes a good serve, that improves her emotional state. At the same time, the way teammates react and respond to a player's success and failure also influences a player's emotional state and potentially her performance.

2. RELEVANCE

When we create learning experiences around leadership skills, it can be challenging to keep these experiences relevant. We can sometimes force the teaching of a certain skill into a sport setting, but it may not work. Ideally, the skill should always match the context; it should not feel forced. For example, Zip, Zap, Boing is effective for developing communication and peer education, but it may not be suitable for teaching anger management. It's better to design a more relevant learning experience in which anger arises more naturally—for example, a challenge that involves physical player-to-player contact or referees who might make bad calls.

3. SEQUENCING

The CSDA Youth Sport Leadership Model follows basic education sequencing techniques—namely, moving from known to unknown, simple to complex, concrete to abstract, and individual to pairs to small groups. Determining which technique to use depends on the purpose and context—what do you want the young people to learn? What knowledge do you want to awaken? Often, it's best to move from simple to more difficult—that is, to start with skills that are easier to master and then modify the experience to make it more challenging. Sometimes, however, it may be better to start with the more difficult skill; it depends on what response we want to facilitate.

For example, resolving a human knot challenge in a large group is much more difficult than with a small group. In fact, in large groups, the task may often seem impossible. We may choose to use the more difficult challenge of unraveling a human knot with a large group for several reasons. For instance, we may want to focus on keeping the entire team united, or we may want to emphasize the importance of perseverance—the idea that anything is possible if we commit to it. Unraveling a large knot may require more time; more maneuvering over, under, around, and through; and more collaboration. But when it's done, the group feels an amazing sense of accomplishment.

On the other hand, we may choose to divide the large

group into smaller groups to do the human knot challenge and have groups compete to see who can unravel the fastest, and then discuss what made the groups complete the challenge successfully. This conversation may lead to themes around collaboration, leadership, problem solving, and so on. You may then choose to increase the difficulty by joining two small groups and repeating the challenge, again debriefing after the challenge to allow participants to learn from the experience. The sequence you use will be guided by what you want to achieve for the specific learning experience.

Similarly, we may choose to engage young people in analysis or reflection that involves moving from individual responses to talking with a partner to sharing with a small group to sharing with the whole group—or vice versa. Starting at the individual level allows for independent thinking without influencing or being influenced by others. On the other hand, starting with the whole group can spark ideas in the individual that can then be explored independently. Both approaches have value—the sequencing format that you choose to use would depend on what you want out of the session.

4. DEVELOPMENTALLY APPROPRIATE

Learning experiences must be age and developmentally appropriate. For example, most eleven-year-olds cannot kick a football as far as an eighteen-year-old, so we need to take that difference into account when designing the challenge. The sport skill might be the same for both age groups—kicking to a goal or passing between partners while running down the field—but the distance between kicker and goal or the distance that partners run down the field should be shorter for the younger age group.

Also, consider the complexity of the challenge. In a learning experience focusing on decision making (leadership skill), this might mean giving the younger players fewer choices. For example, you might tell a group of older teens to come up with a schedule for the tournament. The participants would then decide the number of teams, players per team, time limit of games, type of tournament (single or double elimination, pool play, etc.), and so on; they would create something entirely on their own. With a group of younger kids, you would not leave the challenge so wide open. You might tell the younger ones to create a tournament schedule and limit their choices to option A or option B. The younger ones still have to discuss the options and decide which is best given the number of teams and time/space constraints, but they have a more controlled, developmentally appropriate setting in which to engage in decision making.

Younger children might need more time to come to a decision or work through a challenge. The leadership skill—decision making, for example—doesn't change, but younger groups may take longer to discuss and choose an option.

Even at the younger level, the content should be meaningful—that is, the things they are making decisions about should be real, such as determining the rules that make the most sense based on the given time and space constraints.

When youth are engaged in the challenge, we should be practicing diagnosis and prescription: observing to see if modifications need to be made so the participants truly learn the intended skill. If you realize the participants are struggling, for example, you can add more time and say something like, "You have five more minutes. If you need any help, come and check with me." Likewise, if the participants finish the task quickly, you can end the time early and move on to something else.

The skill can remain constant for all age levels; we can teach serving technique (sports) or anger management (life) or communication (leadership) to eleven-year-olds as well as eighteen-year-olds. The key is designing age-appropriate challenges and using age-appropriate content to awaken the skills. All ages need to learn how to delegate (leadership), but younger kids should be taught in a simpler context: if they're creating a poster, someone can be responsible for the collection and distribution of crayons, someone can collect the finished projects, and so on. This would be too simple for eighteen-year-olds. Instead, we might tell older kids they're in charge of developing, coordinating, and running a promotional campaign to make sports safer for children at their school. They would need to determine what needs to get done and then delegate the various responsibilities.

5. CHALLENGES

To keep young people engaged, the learning experience should become progressively more challenging. In a given session, challenges can be increased as we observe the players' engagement, again using the diagnostic-prescriptive approach. With sport skills, we might increase the challenge halfway through a session by making the target smaller, increasing the shooting distance, or introducing more opponents. With leadership skills, we can make the task more difficult by giving the group more decisions or less time in which to make those decisions. With a life skill such as anger management, we can increase the number of times a player is fouled or gets a bad call or whatever it is that triggers the player's anger.

Challenges should also be increased over the course of a season. In the first part of the season, we might introduce different types of defensive strategies (man marking, zoning, and so on) and have practice sessions for each one.

Later in the season, we might ask the team to determine the strategy they want to use for a particular game, thus increasing the team's decision-making power. Likewise, in the early part of the season, the team might choose a team name and a competition format. Later on, the team might choose offensive and defensive strategies.

The challenges naturally increase as the players move through the phases of the Youth Sport Leadership Model. In the beginning, phase 1, young people learn the concepts and principles; in phase 2, they start practicing those principles with less adult guidance; in phase 3, they apply the principles on their own. At the end, we no longer control the environment; all decisions are made by the young people.

6. VARIETY

To broaden participants' repertoire of experiences and to keep participants engaged, we can add variety in as many situations as possible. This isn't about making challenges harder, just different. For example, if the players are working on shooting accuracy in football, we can add variety by changing the targets—have players shoot to the top right corner of the goal and then to the center of the goal, or change the angle from which they are shooting. We may have them take five consecutive shots at a particular target and then five at another target and so on, or we may have them shoot to a different target and/or from a different angle with each kick. These variations do not necessarily increase the difficulty, but they expand participants' range of experiences for the particular skill, and that variety also makes the activity more engaging.

The same principle applies to the development of leadership skills and life skills. Providing a variety of scenarios that allow young people to explore, apply, and analyze leadership skills such as decision making or life skills such as respect helps to broaden their experiences in each of those skill sets.

Here is an example of adding variety to the decision-making process for the way teams are chosen. We can teach the participants several different ways to pick teams randomly: numbering off, picking names out of a hat, and so on. The group can use the different methods and then discuss the strengths and weaknesses of each. We can also have the group discuss other ways to select teams—for example, the draft system used in the United States.

We often introduce participants to a team selection method for selecting equal-ability teams that involves observation and analysis. We have the young people do an assessment of everyone's skill level. For example, in volleyball all players serve at targets ten times and then receive a score based on the number of times they hit the target; they are also rated on accuracy in passing, setting, and spiking and receive a score for each area. We can do the same for basketball or any other sport.

At the end of the session, the organizing committee (made up of young people) comes together, evaluates the players' scores, and creates teams that are as evenly matched as possible. They select teams based on the objective assessment of skill level and make sure each team has some players who are A level, some who are B level, and some who are C level. This process may be tough for some young people on the committee because they may want to be with their friends, but because they're using an objective scoring system, they will probably end up with other people.

This team selection learning experience is one possible variation that has the potential to provide valuable lessons in objectivity and equity, as well as how and why people make decisions. As mentioned, variety broadens participants' understanding of each skill and how it can be applied, and it also keeps young people meaningfully engaged.

7. GROUP SIZE

Different group sizes work better in different learning experiences. It all comes back to context: the particular group of young people, the goal of the learning experience, whether the group is engaged in the challenge and learning what they should be learning, and so on. Group size options include individual, partner, small group, and large group. Peer work is powerful regardless of whether we're working on a sport skill, life skill, or leadership skill. The one-on-one interaction leads to rich contact, whether it's contact with the ball or with another person. Because it's one-on-one, it's an intense experience.

If peer education is the goal of the learning experience, you might pair strong with weak; the stronger person can help the weaker one. In other cases, partners of equal ability are ideal so the individuals can challenge each other and learn from each other. This applies to groups of three to five as well; sometimes you want a mix of strong and weak, and sometimes you want a group of people who are all on the same level.

The key again is context: What do we want the young people to get out of this learning experience? What group size will best facilitate the outcomes we want? One-on-one pairing provides close interaction and consistent opportunities to contribute because there are only two people involved. A group of five, on the other hand, provides less contact, but it also takes the pressure off each individual because there are more people to interact with. The dynamic is different, but the group is still small enough that the richness of the interaction is not watered down. Groups larger than five provide less interaction opportunities because each person has to wait for five or more people to speak or kick the ball before getting another turn.

We also want to think about the size of group that works for the outcomes we want. A large group is usually best if we want everyone engaged and listening at the same time—for example, if the goal is to communicate simple information that is easy to transfer to the group and doesn't require critical thinking. Sometimes the big-group thing is about unity: we want everyone on the same page. This works with warm-ups, for example, when everyone is doing the same thing. Another reason for the big group is that we might want everyone to hear what one or two or three participants have to say. It's our responsibility as the facilitators to think about the group size that works best for the outcomes we want for that particular session.

The key challenge involves making sure everyone is actively engaged and on task. The larger the group, the longer people have to wait between turns, the less interaction each person gets with any other given player, and the harder it is to make sure everyone stays focused.

> **KEY TAKEAWAYS**
>
> 1. Facilitators should strive to create learning experiences that will lead young people to learn new things rather than learn *about* new things.
>
> 2. Learning experiences should be purpose-driven.
>
> 3. Learning experiences also need to be relevant and contextually appropriate.

CHAPTER 3

Reflecting

Reflection is what distinguishes participating in an activity from engaging in a learning experience. It's true that we learn best by doing, but depth of learning comes when we reflect on what was done or is being done. Reflection is not one final task reserved for the end of a session; it's an ongoing process. When we're engaged in an experience that challenges us to think about a particular skill—whether it's a sport skill, life skill, or leadership skill—we have the opportunity to reflect on what we're learning as we're learning it.

The CSDA model gives participants the opportunity to reflect throughout the experience. Debriefing tools—such as the triangle-square-circle tool mentioned later in this chapter—give young people the chance to gather their insights, analyze them, share them with others, and gain a better understanding and appreciation of the skill being awakened.

THE IMPORTANCE OF REFLECTION

Reflection leads to insight. On one level, young people gain understanding about their own skill development as they reflect individually on what they learned, how they improved, what they could do better next time, and so on. When we facilitate reflection with a partner and in groups, young people gain even more insight, which then leads to innovation. For example, one player might talk about serving technique with another player and realize he could make a change in his own stance.

Reflection also leads to efficiency. Our programs often involve tournaments in which participants take on different leadership roles. At the end of the tournament's first round, the youth administrators meet to debrief about what has happened so far; in other words, they reflect on what has worked well and what hasn't. As they gain insight, they also think about ways to improve to become more efficient. This group reflection leads to innovation, which leads to a better way of organizing the schedule or a better way of handling substitutions, which ultimately leads to a better, more effective tournament.

The same principle applies to other aspects of the tournament—for example, prizes for the winners. The youth administrators meet before the tournament begins; they brainstorm ideas for securing prizes, come to a decision, and apply it. After the tournament, they come back together and reflect on what they did. They decide the approach they used for securing prizes didn't work, so they start brainstorming again. Without this reflection stage, the next tournament would be run using the same method for getting prizes and would generate the same subpar results. Reflection leads to the possibility of finding a better way.

It's common for participants in any kind of activity to complain about something that didn't go smoothly or a rule that didn't make sense. Often, that's where it ends: we complain, but we don't do anything to fix the problem. Through reflection, participants have the opportunity to identify challenges *and* the power to make a change. They think critically about what worked and what didn't, and they come up with possible solutions. That's empowering for young people!

WHEN TO FACILITATE REFLECTION

As facilitators, we have the responsibility to create these reflection opportunities. The goal is to have young people engaged in reflection in all three skill areas: sport, life, and leadership. The reflective process allows youth to continuously find new meaning, new understanding, and new and better ways of doing things to be more efficient and successful.

In the original format of this model, reflection was always done at the end of the program or activity. Now, we include it as an ongoing part of the process, so participants are always in a reflective mode. We don't make this a strict, on-off kind of thing; we don't tell the young people, "OK, start reflecting. OK, stop." The goal is to encourage reflective learners—young people who are always thinking, always learning. We want to develop a reflective culture that permeates the entire program.

At the same time, we do provide specific times to reflect. We design a learning experience to engage the participants, then we add something or take something away to modify the challenge, and then we ask them to think about the whole experience—individually, with a partner, or in a small group, or a combination of all three.

In his talks on leadership, Richard Branson, founder of the Virgin Group, addresses this idea of reflection. He encourages people to forget about taking copious notes during workshops, lectures, and sessions and to instead listen intently, capture in their mind one idea that inspires them, and reflect on that. For our purposes, reflecting goes beyond one idea that inspires, but it is important for young people to really think—to capture in their minds what is being done, to analyze their own actions and the actions of others, to consider innovative ways of doing things. Sometimes this reflection is formal and written; sometimes it's an oral response to a question posed to a group; sometimes it's a direction to take thirty seconds to ponder what happened. The method or methods used depend on the context and the desired result. Structured reflection ideally takes place immediately after the challenge that awakens new knowledge, but as mentioned, the ultimate goal is to create a culture in which young people are continually engaged in reflective learning.

QUESTIONS FOR REFLECTION

Part of reflecting, whether formal or informal, is asking questions to encourage critical thinking and lead young people to key insights. The basic questions we ask may include the following:

- What were some of the challenges you observed? How did you overcome them?
- What did you learn from the activity?
- What would you do differently? Why?

As facilitators, we can also ask more technical questions about specific observations. For example, you might ask players what they noticed about the distance of their kicks or the accuracy of their serves. In relation to leadership skills, you could ask, "What do you think worked well when you delegated tasks to your teammates?" or "What three things helped you use more initiative in this situation?"

These questions are linked to some technical element or principle—a key teaching or coaching point. Asking these technical questions is not enough, however; it's important to take the analysis to the next level, a level that leads to improvement, innovation, or greater efficiency. For example, related to sport skills, you might ask, "Based on your observation, how do you think you could get more distance from your goal kicks?" or "What do you think would be a better way to serve more accurately?" Related to leadership skills, you might ask, "Based on your reflection, how do you think you could communicate to your teammates more clearly?" or "What could you do to come to a decision more quickly?"

With these improvement-related questions, young people not only consider what they just did; they also reflect on things they could have done differently to be more effective. These questions lead to innovation and creativity. For example, after the program tournament, youth administrators might ask themselves, "What could we have done to make the schedule more user friendly?" or "How could we have drafted the teams in a way that was more equitable?" These questions lead participants to reflect on what they did, how they did it, and what they learned from it, as well as what they could do to improve.

Another dimension or level of reflecting involves asking *why*. If one of the youth referees wasn't as calm as she should have been, you as the facilitator could ask, "Why do you think you lost your cool?" Or if a young person wasn't serving accurately during an activity, you could ask, "Why do you think your serve kept going off to the left?" Or if someone didn't complete tasks that had been delegated to her, you could ask, "Why do you think that happened?" Asking *why* doesn't give room for excuses; it encourages the young person to consider her actions and discover the root reason behind them.

The lowest level of questioning involves asking *what* happened; that generates a retelling of the facts, which is important, but it's not as powerful as analyzing *why* something happened. When we ask why, we encourage deeper thinking, innovation, and real change.

THE FACILITATOR'S ROLE

The two key roles for the facilitator are to provide opportunities for reflection and to help young people develop an appreciation for the value of reflecting. The tools and methods we use to encourage reflection vary depending on the program and its specific goals, but there are some overarching guidelines that may be useful regardless of the context.

One general principle is that we shouldn't judge participants' reflective statements. We can ask for clarification and build on comments, but we don't want to evaluate their responses as good or bad. Our job is to provide opportunities for reflection and then listen and understand what the young people learned from the experience. There is value to doing this activity as a group for five minutes; hearing others' answers will get the ideas flowing for those who are stuck.

Another guideline is that we also want to provide opportunities for all kinds of reflection—individual, paired, small group, and whole group, as well as written and spoken—and provide various tools with which to do that thinking. We want to give young people plenty of practice so that reflective learning becomes a valued natural habit.

Finally, we can vary the content of the reflection according to the context of the program. With more structured reflections, we can ask participants to write about one specific domain—the one awakened in the preceding challenge—or we can leave it open and let young people decide if they want to consider sport skills, life skills, or leadership skills. At the end of a session in a leadership program, for example, you might ask young people to reflect on the specific leadership skill they encountered through that day's challenging activity. Or you might ask about the sport skill they learned. Or the life skill. It all depends on the context and what we want to achieve through that specific learning experience.

WRITTEN AND SPOKEN REFLECTION

Although we do have young people share their reflections verbally, we also encourage writing. We find there's a stronger connection when people write down their thoughts. We urge young people to have their own notebooks and to use these for recording their observations. We also facilitate conversations about the ideas they have written down. Writing cements understanding. It gives youth something to go back to, read over, and reflect on further.

It is important to keep the written task simple. If young people see the reflective practice as complicated or difficult, they are not likely to think it's worth the effort; we want them to view reflection as valuable and as something they can practice regularly in just a few minutes. The end goal of the leadership program is transference of skills from the sport/physical education setting into everyday life. Likewise, we want young people to take this reflective practice skill beyond the learning experience itself and use it in any space of learning, whether it's a classroom, a job, or a church. Anytime they are engaged in experiences that have potential to facilitate new thinking, we want them to embrace the reflective process.

One simple activity we use to help participants use written and spoken reflection is the triangle-square-circle (TSC) tool (figure 3.1). The TSC reflection tool may be used for reflections on leadership skills, sport skills, or life skills that are being facilitated through the learning experience. Each shape represents a different reflection focus:

- Triangle: What are three key points about the topic that you learned?
- Square: What are four things that squared up with your beliefs/understanding?
- Circle: What questions or thoughts are swirling around in your mind?

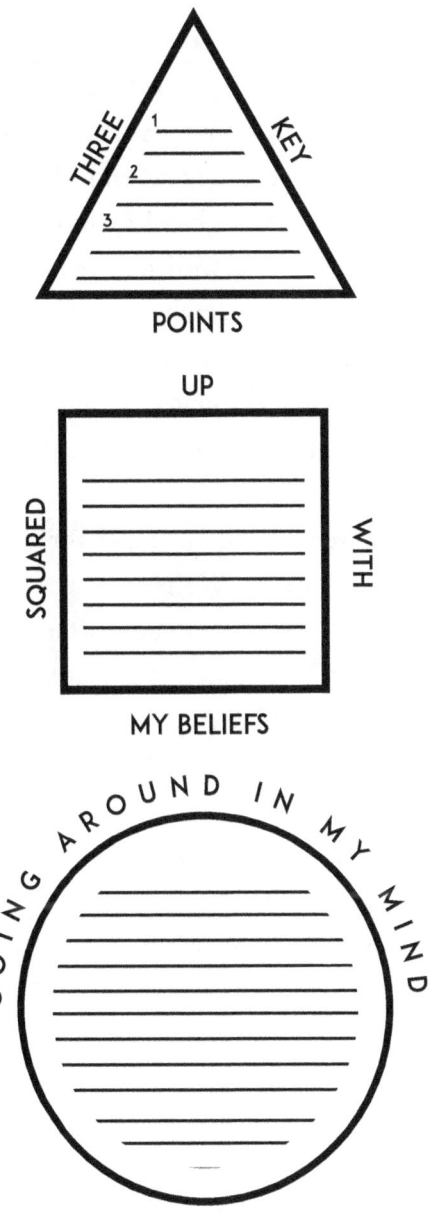

Figure 3.1: TSC Reflection Tool

The triangle has three sides, so it naturally suggests writing about three key points; likewise for the square and writing about four things. However, these are not hard-and-fast rules. Depending on the context and what we want the participants to learn, we might ask for just one key point or two things that squared up with their beliefs. Or we might ask them to brainstorm as many lessons as they can and then pick their top three. Once again, it all depends on the focus of that particular learning experience. The TSC tool is just that—a tool to be used to achieve the desired end.

In most cases, we start the sequence for using the TSC tool at the individual level. We have each participant write down their responses immediately after the challenge, starting with the triangle, then the square, and finally the circle. By reflecting and writing individually first, young people are not influenced by other participants' answers.

Then individuals pair up and talk about their responses. This isn't just sharing; it's a conversation to ask questions and learn from each other. This helps participants take their reflections to the next level. Sharing ideas is how we grow. We learn how other people think; we learn that some people have very similar experiences and others are completely different. The more conversations young people have and the more people who are collectively engaged in the thinking process, the wider variety of perspectives they are exposed to and can learn from.

Next, we might have two pairs join each other and so on. This sequence often produces a richer conversation because each individual has taken time to reflect and can participate in the larger group discussion. Often when sequencing starts at the large-group level, a few strong personalities dominate the conversation, and even if everyone has a chance to share, the ideas shared by the strong individuals tend to be the most popular.

If you want to trigger as many ideas as possible first and then have participants reflect on these, following a larger group-to-individual sequence works better. This order helps people who might not fully understand the process or know what kinds of things they should be thinking about. Someone might mention an idea that another person hadn't considered, and this may trigger more ideas in the second person's mind. The appropriate sequence all depends on context.

To get the whole group involved in sharing, we sometimes use a different approach. Instead of filling out the TSC at the end of a session, young people take it home. When they come in the next day, they post their reflections on a board (anonymously) and then walk around and look at everyone else's posts. We often do this as a silent "museum walk"; there's no conversation, but there's a powerful interaction with what other young people have written. They learn from one another. One viewer might look at another person's tool and think, *Wow, I didn't consider that.* After the silent viewing, we have a whole-group conversation and anyone can contribute. Each person is helped by being meaningfully engaged together in the reflective process. They learn from others, and they also learn from themselves. As youth talk through their own reflections, they awaken nuggets of knowledge that they already possess. It's a powerful process.

As facilitators, we want participants to understand, value, and appreciate the reflective process. After using the TSC reflection tool, for example, you might ask participants to share their thoughts about the tool itself—challenges with and usefulness of the tool, how it may be improved to better capture their thoughts and ideas, and any other ideas about the TSC tool and the process of using it. In a sense, you're helping them reflect about reflecting, and by doing so, you're building an appreciation for the value of the reflective process.

KEY TAKEAWAYS

1. Young people learn best by doing when they reflect on what was done.

2. The facilitator's role is to give young people the tools and opportunities to reflect.

3. As young people share their reflections, they awaken nuggets of knowledge they already have stored.

CHAPTER 4

The Facilitator's Role

In the CSDA model, we see the coach/teacher as a facilitator, not an information provider. As facilitators, we don't own the knowledge that we share with the young people; instead, we facilitate the awakening of knowledge the participants already possess. Primarily, in the context of this book, our role is to facilitate the awakening of leadership skills.

This role has another level, too. As we facilitate, we also model the very leadership skills we want the young people to demonstrate. It's a dynamic relationship.

THE ROLE OF THE COACH/TEACHER AS YOUTH LEADERSHIP FACILITATOR

At CSDA, we have found the following guidelines helpful in executing our role in youth leadership development.

1. WE ARE FACILITATORS, NOT INFORMATION DELIVERERS

Children have access to all the information we do; they can Google things just as easily as we can. Instead of dumping declarative content on youth, we want to awaken knowledge they already have by getting them to think and reflect. And we do that by engaging them in challenging learning experiences. A key part of the facilitator's role is designing effective learning experiences that awaken, or facilitate the awakening of, leadership skills through sport.

2. WE DESIGN EXPERIENCES AND OBSERVE THEIR EFFECTIVENESS

For learning to happen, young people need to be engaged in the learning experience. Our responsibility is to constantly observe the young people to ensure that they are meaningfully engaged and that they are gaining the intended knowledge. If not, we ask ourselves why: Is the challenge too easy? Is it too difficult? Is it too boring or too immature?

If the challenge is not generating the intended outcome,

we may need to intervene: we may stop the activity and make adjustments to either increase or decrease the difficulty, or we may add a new dimension or clarify the guidelines. If young people are going to gain leadership skills, knowledge, and practice, we need to ensure that the learning experiences that we design actually lead to those outcomes. We can't let ineffective sessions continue unchanged; we must be willing to stop the challenge if necessary and make modifications.

3. WE FACILITATE SUCCESS

The CSDA model is a success-based approach: we want youth to be successful, so we modify the environment in our sport-based learning experiences to help youth experience success.

Some people disagree with this approach, saying that real life isn't like that; real life is more like the school of hard knocks. But this is a success-*based* approach; it doesn't mean youth will always be successful. A main goal is to help them view success as improvement and not so much as winning. We modify activities so youth experience success in various ways, as individuals and as teams, in actual games and in simple activities.

For example, if we're working on the sports skill of serving a volleyball, we might design an experience that involves serving to targets. To do so, we set up nets along the court, rather than across the court, so we can have more teams lined up side by side. We divide the group into teams of four, and the teams line up single file with the first person from each team standing behind the serving line, facing the net. On the other side of the net, we place a hoop. Each person serves toward the hoop. If the ball goes into the hoop, that team gets a point. After a player serves, he retrieves his ball and gets back in line behind his teammates. Meanwhile, the next person on his team serves, and then goes to retrieve his ball, and so on. The activity continues for one minute. At the end, the facilitator blows the whistle and asks each team for their total score.

Even though one team scored the most points and "won," we don't even mention it. We want everyone to succeed, so we control the environment to help everyone feel successful. We might say, "We're going to do this again. Let's see if your team can beat your first score." And then we blow the whistle and let them start. As facilitators, we're focused on the team that scored the fewest points the first time. If that team scored ten points, for example, we'll keep the game going until they score twelve points and then blow the whistle, even if we have to go over the one-minute time limit. The participants aren't aware that we have gone over one minute. They're not aware that we've manipulated the environment to give that team a sense of success.

Some people frown on this approach because they think it doesn't prepare children for the real world. However, we see it as context. In that learning experience context, we want all participants to feel successful. In another learning context, we might want all participants to feel challenged. We might shorten the time of the second game and then say to a team, "Wait. You got fifteen the first time. How come you got only ten? What could you have done differently?" In this way, we're challenging them to think about how they can score faster.

Everything is contextual. As facilitators, we need to know what we want out of the learning experiences we design and make adjustments/manipulations accordingly. Sometimes we want our athletes to feel success, and sometimes we want them to feel challenged. Facilitating is part art and part science.

Knowing when and how to modify a challenge also requires knowing the young people with whom we work. We need to have a relationship with them. We need to understand them, so that we know when to push and when to pull, when to challenge and when to help them succeed.

This concept also applies to communicating leadership skills. If the youth administrators write up a tournament schedule and bring it to you, and you see lots of mistakes, you have a couple of options. You could say, "This is no good. You made a mess of this." Or you could say, "Good effort. Tell me why you did this. How could you have done this better?" The second response uses a success-based approach that facilitates their growth and improvement, rather than just criticizing and telling them to redo it.

At the same time, there might come a point when you challenge them and say, "Hey, come on. You can do a little better. Remember that thing we talked about? Where can you find that information? OK. Go back with your group and try again." Again, facilitating is part art and part science—knowing the delicate balance between facilitating their success and challenging them to improve.

It's important to remember that success is not just winning; it's about improvement. In activities like the volleyball drill, we don't ask for or acknowledge the winner in terms of highest score. We're looking for success in terms of progress, both as individuals and as teams.

4. WE ENCOURAGE REFLECTION THROUGHOUT THE LEARNING EXPERIENCE

As discussed in chapter 3, we want to create a culture of continual reflection. At different points during the volleyball drill, for example, we can help participants think about more than just serving at a target; we might ask them to think about where their front foot is placed—for instance, is it pointed at the target?—or whether they take a breath before they serve. Sometimes we need to ask specific questions about these things to get youth thinking and to get them to the lesson we want them to learn from the experience. For example, you might ask, "What are you doing with that front foot? What are you looking at when you're serving?" And after the activity is over, you might ask, "What were you looking at when your serves were most accurate?" We don't tell them the answers; we lead them in the right direction so they make the discovery on their own.

We also want participants to think about the challenge itself, including any modifications we make. We do this by asking young people to analyze their performance. For example, in the previous volleyball drill, you might ask, "Did your score improve? What did you do differently the second time? What do you think was responsible for the change?" We can encourage young people to have this conversation among themselves, too. We don't always have to be part of the discussion.

5. WE PROVIDE A HIGH-QUALITY SPORT EXPERIENCE

As facilitators, we must understand the basics of good coaching, accurate sport skills development, and best practices on the playing field—no matter what skills are being presented in our program. We cannot have the attitude, "Oh, we're working on communication skills; it doesn't matter if the players use poor technical skills." Whether the program is designed to awaken life skills such as patience or leadership skills such as initiative, the sport component itself must be high quality and authentic. A rich sport experience is integral to the success of the CSDA model, and it starts with us.

UNDERSTANDING YOUNG PEOPLE

As mentioned, understanding young people is key to knowing when and how to modify a given challenge. Part of understanding young people is recognizing that they all have different strengths and different capabilities; this applies to the context of life skills and leadership skills, as well as sport skills. Some people are better at shooting, and some are better at passing; some people control their anger better, and others know how to show respect; some people have great communication skills, and others are better at delegating. When working with young people, we should remember these differences and avoid forcing everyone to do the same activity just because it's on our agenda. We need to understand the young people we're working with and tailor our programs to their needs and strengths.

Just as everyone has strengths in different areas, we all

have areas where we're not as strong. When we're faced with participating in something we don't think we can do, we might feel nervous and unsure. This happens on the individual, team, group, and organization level. Our fear often stems from focusing on what we don't have or can't do—for example, we don't have experience organizing that kind of competition, or we've never run that distance. The key is to start with what we have and build up to the activity we're faced with. When working with young people, we can ask, "What do you do well? What strength can we build on?" And again, we don't want to force all young people into the same skill or learning timetable. It may take some longer to build up confidence to swim in the deep end of the pool or take on a bigger task in organizing a tournament.

In order to build on the strengths our players have, we have to know what those strengths are. And the key to knowing their strengths is knowing our young people and building relationships with them. Here are some key elements to understanding young people and building these relationships.

1. WHAT ARE THEY THINKING?

It's important to know what individual young people are thinking, because they're not all thinking the same thing. How do we learn what they're thinking? As facilitators, we create a space that allows them to share. That space isn't necessarily physical in the sense that we give them a platform or structured time to share. We create an atmosphere in which young people feel comfortable being who they are and saying what they're really thinking. Otherwise, they will just try to be what we expect or what we have already pegged them as. If we think they are negative and stubborn, they will be negative and stubborn. In their minds, the reasoning goes something like this: "Oh well, Coach already thinks I can't play football, so I'm not gonna be any good." From their perspective, we've already set the expectation, and they'll be what we want them to be—or worse.

Our responsibility is to create a youth-friendly space where they feel comfortable being themselves and where they feel comfortable sharing. The sport setting is perfect for doing that because it is authentic and real; young people tend to let down their guard when they're involved in sport and let others see who they really are.

> ### SAFEGUARDING CHILDREN IN SPORTS
>
> Facilitating the development of leadership requires the creation of a safe, youth-friendly environment. Because of the authentic nature of sport, that environment is also vulnerable at times. As children engage in sport and develop relationships, they share more openly than they might in other settings. This is a positive thing, but it also creates an opportunity for abuse on several levels. It is our responsibility as coaches, physical education teachers, and community volunteers to provide a positive sport experience and to safeguard children from all forms of harm. To find out more about how you can make sport safer for children and young people, check out the International Safeguards at https://www.sportanddev.org/en/learn-more/child-protection-and-safeguarding-sport.

2. WHAT DO THEY WANT?

In a youth-friendly space, coaches and teachers should be willing to learn from young people. We can find out what they want—both on an individual and group level.

Adults sometimes think all young people are the same—they want the same things, enjoy the same activities, and so on. In reality, young people are people, and each one of them is an individual with individual likes and dislikes; we need to treat them as such.

In terms of leadership development through sport, we need to remember that not all young people want to be engaged in sports. Some might be interested in the scores and statistics aspect or in officiating but not in actually playing.

As facilitators, educators, and coaches, we want to encourage participation in physical activities for their many health and social benefits. But not everyone wants to run one hundred meters or play football. So the challenge is creating an experience youth want to take part in. We want to encourage participation in some physical activity, but we don't want to force them to play a certain sport such as cricket or basketball. To a certain extent, for the purposes of leadership development through sport, it doesn't matter what they play; what matters is that they are fully engaged in the activity, and this is more likely to happen if the activity is something they want to do.

3. HOW ARE THEY ENGAGED?

We respect that some individuals don't want to be on the volleyball team or basketball team, and we can seek to accommodate those preferences. This isn't about giving in to the whims of every individual child; we can't realistically have forty children doing forty different activities because they can't agree on a single game. But we can have a conversation with the youth, find out what they want, and give them choices. In this way, we're respecting their interests and needs and also awakening an appreciation of the need for physical activity. If we are effective in this, we should be able to get the young people engaged and benefiting.

As a leader in youth sport, you recognize its value in facilitating the development of healthy lifestyle habits, as well as social and leadership skills. The goal is to impart this same appreciation to young people in an indirect, thoughtful way—not in an imposing, old-school way that says, "Everyone has to participate in gym class, and this is what we're all doing today."

THE IMPORTANCE OF LISTENING

I learned the importance of listening through a humbling experience. A few years ago, I participated in a facilitation workshop put on by the UK-based company MTa. I was seeking to improve my facilitation skills, which would help in our work training teachers and coaches and in developing youth leadership through sport in general. When I arrived in London, I learned a harsh lesson: I was not a very good facilitator.

I've been in teacher education for a long time, and I usually get positive reviews. I thought I was pretty good at it. So when I was asked to lead a session at the MTa workshop, I said yes. It was a small group of about ten people from all different sectors: airline industry, banking, and so on. I was the only one from a nonprofit. As I facilitated the session, I listened to everyone's responses and used a flipchart to summarize the dialogue with diagrams, arrows, and so on. I thought I did a fantastic job.

After the session, I had a one-on-one meeting with the lead facilitator, and it was harsh. I learned that one of my greatest weaknesses is listening. I also learned that I am strongly opinionated (I think I already knew that!). I thought I had captured the small-group conversation on the chart, but in reality, I captured only my perspective and my opinion of the group conversation. The things I highlighted in the summary and through my dialogue facilitation reflected my biased ideas. I felt like an old shoe after my one-on-one, but it taught me that I needed to be a better listener.

For the rest of that week, my main task was listening and then summarizing what I heard without making any judgment. It was an eye-opening learning experience. In particular, it gave me an appreciation of the importance of listening in the context of working with young people. We can't just half listen to them; we need to give them our full attention. When we don't listen intently and without distraction, we miss nuances of what they're saying and how they're saying it. And when we miss it, it's gone. You can't reread it like a book; if you're not listening carefully and you miss something, it doesn't come back.

As a result of my humbling experience, we now use more

deliberate listening in our CSDA programs. We encourage coaches and teachers to watch the young people they're working with, to look at their facial expressions and pick up on their emotions through what is unspoken. That's all part of the dialogue and what the young people are trying to communicate.

By listening deliberately and nonjudgmentally and by watching young people as they speak, we come to understand them better and build relationships with them. At the same time, as we model deliberate listening toward youth, young people in turn learn this important life skill. Youth need to be good listeners with their peers and with their teammates; later in life, they will need to be good listeners with their workmates, friends, and spouses.

In our programs, we use several tasks to facilitate this listening. For example, at the end of a session we summarize what the young people have contributed. We also use partner work, so that each person is listening intently to what his or her partner is sharing and then the roles switch and the other person practices listening. The key in each activity is learning to listen for meaning.

MEANINGFUL CONVERSATIONS

Listening is part of having meaningful conversations. The importance of such conversations is sometimes overlooked—not just in the leadership development context but in life in general. When we don't have meaningful conversations, relationships and teams can fall apart. A key book on this topic that we've used in our organization, training workshops, and youth programs is *Crucial Conversations*.[3]

Young people have their own challenges—at school, at home, online through social media—but adults don't know what's happening if they don't engage youth in meaningful conversations. And if we don't know what's going on in young people's lives or what they're thinking, we can't help them.

As coaches in a team setting, we have a responsibility to facilitate these meaningful conversations to address issues. For example, you might have an individual who starts falling to the fringe; he stops adding value to the team and actually becomes more of a disruption to the group's performance, whether because he storms off the field during practice or disrupts a tournament-planning activity or some other situation. Your responsibility as a facilitator is twofold: you facilitate a meaningful conversation with the player and you model this leadership behavior to your team.

---

3   Kerry Patterson, Al Switzler, Joseph Grenny, and Ron McMillan, *Crucial Conversations: Tools for Talking When Stakes Are High*, 2nd ed. (New York: McGraw Hill, 2012).

The meaningful conversation starts with sharing information. If someone walks off, we don't judge him; we start by asking, "What's going on?" In that friendly, nonjudgmental space, the young person can explain why he stormed off the field. Now we understand the reason behind his action and we can say, "OK. I didn't realize that you didn't get much to do during this activity," or whatever it is.

Having a meaningful conversation starts the movement toward behavior adjustment. And as we're having the conversation, we're teaching a leadership skill—we're weaving knowledge into young people by using the communication process with them. We're facilitating this opportunity to share what's happening—the reason behind their behavior—but we can only do this if we have a relationship with the young people, if we listen, and if we have provided a friendly, nonjudgmental space. If we ask a player why he stormed off the field and he says because he's feeling left out and ignored, we don't respond with something judgmental like, "Well, how can you feel that?" We just want to listen. Then in response, we can share our perspective—not defending, not challenging, just sharing: "OK, thanks for sharing. Now I understand. Here's what I was thinking when you stormed off."

The result is that both parties now have all of the information; *Crucial Conversations* calls this the pool of shared information. Now the facilitator knows, for example, that the player didn't storm off because he was mad at John but because he had a headache. Based on this conversation and the pool of shared information, we can now make decisions that lead to a resolution and behavior adjustment.

On any team and in any group activity, no matter what level—from a hopscotch team on the playground to the champion's league football team—there will be challenges that require resolution. As facilitators, we must not ignore these conflicts; they will not just go away. We have a responsibility to address the challenge by engaging the young people in a meaningful conversation, by asking questions in a nonjudgmental way so we can come to a shared pool of information about the situation and then make decisions about how to resolve it.

Sometimes these conversations will be one-on-one, as in the previous example. Sometimes, however, you might have a whole team or group that is not interacting, and this needs to be addressed as well. You might initiate the group conversation as the facilitator, or you might let someone on the team do it, someone who has strong listening and communication skills. If you're working on delegation skills, you might let the team captain delegate the task to someone (in section two, we present delegation as one of the key leadership skills). Either way, the group conversation should be conducted in a nonjudgmental atmosphere of information sharing with the goal being some kind of truce, some solution that will prevent the negative group dynamic from deteriorating further.

THE DIAGNOSTIC-PRESCRIPTIVE APPROACH

As facilitators, we need to remember that we're dealing with individuals; the skills we present should be appropriate for the group and people we're working with. We want to present information those specific participants need.

Before we start working with a group of young people, we need to learn what they already know and the skills they already have; this is the *diagnostic* part of the approach. After we diagnose, then we can determine what knowledge we can reinforce, what skill can be developed further, what problem we can correct, and so on; this is the *prescriptive* part of the approach. The diagnostic-prescriptive approach to skills development applies to all three domains: sport skills, life skills, and leadership skills.

It is important to understand the context within which we're presenting skills. In this case, we're working with young people, and we need to diagnose what they need before we can accurately prescribe—and even then, we are not prescribing. Rather than jump in and say, "OK, I noticed that you're not really good at this skill," we have a conversation with the young people and ask, "Where are you? What do you think you need to work on most?"

In using this diagnostic-prescriptive approach, we are not teaching or telling or dictating. We're facilitating a better understanding of what skills and knowledge the young people already have as well as what types of experiences we need to design to facilitate the awakening of the skills they need and want. We might start with a self-assessment or self-audit, something like that presented in Hellison's model of Teaching Personal and Social Responsibility (see figure 4.1 for an example of the CSDA Life Skill Assessment Matrix). We might ask, "Where are you? Are you at the lowest level? The middle level? Where do you want to be?" The young people then conduct their own self-assessment and determine where they are with regard to the skill being discussed and where they want to be. Someone might say, "I want to move from being responsible to being very responsible" or "I am somewhat caring, but I want to be more caring toward other people." Our responsibility is to design the learning experience that will move the young people from where they are to where they want to be.

LIFE SKILLS ASSESSMENT MATRIX: RESPECT

NAME: _____

DATE: _____

RESPECT FOR SELF	NEVER	SOMETIMES	MOST TIMES	ALWAYS
Takes care of oneself by keeping clean and tidy				
Makes smart food choices and avoids harmful drugs				
Participates in regular physical activity				
Maintains strong commitment to learning/development and acheivement of goals				

RESPECT FOR OTHERS				
Actively listens to others and considers their point of view				
Works cooperatively with others				
Apologizes when he/she makes mistakes or offends others				
Appreciates other people's differences (including religious, ethnic, gender, disability, etc.)				
Demonstrates equity in interactions with others regardless of differences.				

RESPECT FOR PROPERTY				
Takes good care of personal property and belongings				
Respects other people's spaces and property (not invading or using without permission)				
Does not litter or deface public spaces/property				
Demonstrates care for the environment				

Figure 4.1: Example of a CSDA Life Skill Assessment Matrix

We usually keep the assessment levels simple: *low* means not achieving, *middle* means in progress, and *high* means the person has achieved the skill. Then we might have them assess themselves on four different leadership skills (or life skills or sport skills, whatever the focus is): for example, decision making, communication, resourcefulness, and delegation. A young person might say, "When it comes to delegating, I'm in the middle—work in progress. But in decision making, I'm not doing so well."

When we do youth programs, we usually administer an individual survey so we know whom we're working with. These surveys also give us an idea of the literacy level as well as some of the content experiences in all three domains: sports, life, and leadership. Sometimes we do peer assessment or facilitator assessment instead of self-assessment, but even in these cases, the individuals must agree with the assessment; in other words, they have the final say in where they are with regard to a certain skill and where they want to end up.

Sometimes we also do team assessments or audits, where the team as a whole decides what to work on. For example, in terms of sport skills, team members might decide that their offense is great, but their defense is weak, or they might say that they are in great physical shape but have poor technique. In terms of leadership skills, they might say they have great teamwork, but their individual resourcefulness is lacking. In terms of life skills, they might say they show respect to the referees, but they don't manage anger well toward the other team. As facilitators, we design experiences to help players meet their goals—as individuals, teams, and the whole group.

We can assess many dimensions, but these should be informed by listening to the young people, not based on our agenda. Using this diagnostic-prescriptive approach is more meaningful. It's based on the particular needs and wants of the group in front of us. It gives a proper assessment of where an individual, group, or team stands and where they want to be, and based on that information, we can design experiences to move them forward.

In the midst of a learning experience, the facilitator might discover that the desired end is not being achieved. Maybe the participants found the task too easy or too hard, or maybe it's not awakening the skill in the desired way. Rather than continue the experience, the facilitator should make adjustments. Sometimes this means tweaking the existing activity, and sometimes it means trying something completely different. The important thing is to stop doing what's not working and make adjustments to get to where the young people want to be.

> **KEY TAKEAWAYS**
>
> 1. The facilitation of youth sport leadership is both an art and a science.
>
> 2. Careful listening is a prerequisite for understanding young people's needs.
>
> 3. Diagnosis and prescription is a valuable approach to ensure that we engage people on the basis of their needs.

SECTION TWO

Developing Leadership Skills

I credit a great deal of my own personal development to the years I spent as a student of Presentation College in San Fernando (the equivalent of a US high school)—possibly the only college in the world to produce two prime ministers, one president, several government ministers, and many leaders in medicine, law, industry, music, sport, and commerce. The college has a strong ethos of leadership development that is embedded in the overall culture of the institution and that provides opportunities for students to develop leadership in a wide range of authentic settings.

One such setting is the 1st Presentation Sea Scouts, a scout troop that focuses on water activities. During my time as a student at the college, I joined the scout troop under the leadership of then principal Brother Michael Samuel. Brother Michael used a teaching style similar to what we're presenting in this book; that is, rather than tell us what to do, he gave us challenges within a controlled environment and let us figure out the solutions. In the process, we learned key leadership skills.

The scout troop, like many other organized groups at the college, used a peer education approach: as boys learned skills, they in turn taught others, rather than having adults do the instructing. Peer education started right away; for example, as twelve- and thirteen-year-olds mastered swimming, rowing, knot tying, and orienteering, they taught the incoming eleven-year-olds these skills. The seventeen- and eighteen-year-olds, in turn, led the entire scout troop. These senior boys planned and conducted troop meetings, organized hikes and camps, and so on, with minimal adult intervention.

The scout troop of around forty boys was divided into five groups, or patrols, with a leadership hierarchy within each patrol—from the youngest and newest scouts up to the patrol leader, who was usually fifteen or sixteen years old. Each patrol was given a significant amount of autonomy in terms of decision making. For example, if the troop was going camping, each patrol would come up with a menu for the five-day camp and they would determine what food and equipment needed to be brought along: pots and pans for cooking, tools for setting up tents, and so on. Patrols even did their own grocery shopping. The only adult intervention was transportation to the campsite, because we usually camped in some faraway location in the bush. After dropping off scouts at the campsite, the adults would leave, and the troop functioned on its own, under the leadership of the senior boys, also known as venture scouts.

In one of these camps, I was the only venture scout. I was seventeen years old, and I was in charge of a group of thirty to forty boys camping out on a series of tiny islands off the northwestern peninsula of Trinidad; the only way to get there is by boat. During that camp, the school principal and scout leader (Brother Michael) and a few parents visited us on campfire night, but other than that, there was no adult intervention or supervision for the entire week.

This was an amazing experience for me. As the venture scout in charge, I was in an authentic leadership role; I had learned the skills to execute this role through the culture of the scout troop. From a young age, I was given opportunities to make decisions and to lead with limited adult intervention. As I was involved in the patrols on camp trips, I was given challenges—cooking, navigating, hiking, swimming, rowing, and so on. All of these experiences required teamwork, and they all involved real, authentic challenges: if we didn't cook, we didn't eat; if we couldn't put up our tent and build our campsite, we didn't live comfortably for a week.

The lesson here is that when we give young people the opportunity to lead in authentic situations—whether in a scout, sport, or other youth-based group setting—they have the potential to learn leadership skills they will use for life. There are many skills that add value to one's leadership capacity. In this section, we present eight key skills that form the foundation for solid leadership development—**communication, teamwork, resourcefulness, adaptability, delegation, decision making, initiative, and getting things done**—and we provide suggestions for developing them in the sport setting. Implicit in communicating and developing each of these skills are the overarching principles outlined in section one.

> **REMINDER: THE THREE OVERARCHING PRINCIPLES**
>
> 1. Awaken knowledge in participants.
> 2. Facilitate experiences to reinforce and practice that knowledge.
> 3. Encourage reflection on those experiences.

CHAPTER 5

Communication

Communication is a skill for life, beyond the playing field and beyond a designated leadership setting. We all communicate on a daily basis, at all levels, our whole lives; we communicate with friends, siblings, spouses, children, teachers, coaches, coworkers, employers, and more. On a global scale, world leaders speak with each other and with the citizens of their respective countries; communication plays a big part in the relationships between whole nations. In the Caribbean, for example, countries meet as one region or community. When leaders of the individual territories change, the relationships between the countries as a whole may change, and it has nothing to do with national policy; it has to do with personality and communication skills and how people get along.

Despite its lifelong importance, communication is often

overlooked in the school setting and is not taught with deliberation in the same way that math and science are. As coaches and teachers, we have an opportunity to awaken critical elements of communication in youth—elements that facilitate and improve relationships between individuals, groups, and whole countries.

Communication is a platform for building relationships. The reality is that we live among other people; we work together, live together, and play together. These relationships can be improved, both in terms of efficiency and enjoyment, if we engage in effective and meaningful communication.

In terms of leadership, communication is closely related to many of the other skills discussed in this section. Leaders must communicate effectively to improve teamwork, decision making, and more.

KEY DIMENSIONS OF COMMUNICATION

In our work with young people, we consider communication in terms of three broad dimensions:

1. Respect: Communicating respectfully in the context of building relationships
2. Perception and awareness: Communicating as it relates to perception and awareness—both of self and of others

3. Mechanics: Communicating clearly and effectively to ensure accuracy and understanding

These three dimensions interact with each other in varying degrees during the process of communicating; we consider them as separate dimensions only for the purpose of understanding them better. In this section, we also present learning experiences we use to facilitate a greater understanding of communication skills among young people.

RESPECT

Respect is one of the most important parts of communication. No matter what the topic or who is involved in the conversation, communication by all involved should be respectful. In our work with young people, we provide learning experiences that help young people consider what it looks like when we speak with respect.

One such experience involves a regular deck of playing cards. The deck should have a mix of high cards—kings, queens, and jacks—and low cards, as well as a joker. We shuffle the deck and then give each participant a card. As soon as participants receive a card, they hold it up to their foreheads without looking at it. The number or picture on the card should be facing out so others in the group can see it. Then the young people walk around the room exchanging greetings with each other based on the number or picture on the other person's card. For example, if participant A walks up to someone with a queen, participant A's greeting will demonstrate respect or graciousness or whatever would be appropriate for greeting a queen. Likewise, participants should greet someone holding a joker in a way that suggests the picture on the card but doesn't say it outright.

After a certain amount of time, we ask people to move into different areas of the room according to what they think their card is based on the way other people greeted them. We might say, "If you think you have a high card, stand over here; if you think you have a low card, over there; if you think you have the joker, stand here; and if you're not sure, stand over there." It's interesting to listen to participants explain why they think they have the card they do. For example, the people with high cards often say things such as, "People bowed down to me and saluted me." People with low cards usually feel like people looked down on them. We have had people holding the joker get truly offended because people laughed at them.

This activity enables quality conversation about communication and how we interact with people based on what we see. To encourage reflection after the experience, we ask questions such as, "What is important about how we greet people? Do we greet someone with respect because they wear a crown? How do we treat people who are wearing shabby clothes? Do we treat them with respect, the way we would treat someone wearing a crown?"

We also discuss social interaction aspects of communication. For example, the person holding the joker sometimes feels humiliated because people laughed at her. We draw the connection to real-life situations where we might laugh at someone or something the person said, but the individual didn't intend it as a joke and doesn't appreciate being laughed at. We might ask the group, "How do you know when you have offended someone and what do you do when you realize it? How do you respond?" This works the other way around, too. We ask the group if they like being treated like a king and if they think it's OK if someone bows down to another person in greeting.

We then prompt participants to think about these social aspects of communication in a sport and team setting. For example, the player who wears the number 10 jersey in football is often looked up to as the star player. We ask the group how they respond to this person away from the team setting, say, in the halls at school, compared to one of the players who isn't as skilled. Do they give the star player a high five but ignore the other player? We also ask participants how they would feel, both as the player who is being bypassed in the hall and as the player doing the bypassing. We sometimes ask the same questions regarding how people treat overweight players versus physically fit players or really tall players versus short players.

This activity focuses on respect in communication, but we don't tell young people that up front. As facilitators, we don't prescribe what we want participants to discuss at the end. We pose questions and prompt them to reflect on communication and the different dynamics involved—respect, social class, judging people based on color or status or clothes. In most cases, young people come up with the idea that communication with everyone should be respectful.

Respectful communication initiates the establishment of trust and is the foundation for building relationships. As mentioned in the introduction, the sport setting provides an authentic setting for relationship building and is thus the perfect place to work on respectful communication. Our role as coaches and teachers is to facilitate a deeper appreciation of the value of communicating respectfully. We want young people to think about the level of respect they exhibit when they communicate with individuals in various roles, with various outward appearance: Do they perceive different value based on appearances? Do they communicate more or less respectfully based on those value judgments? Through the learning experiences we design, we want to awaken an appreciation for respectful communication with all, both on and off the field, in a nonjudgmental way.

Responding to Disrespectful or Negative Communication

Because the sport setting is vulnerable and people tend to let down their guard, disrespectful conversation happens at all levels—from professional to grassroots settings for both adults and youth. In our sport-based programs, we want to develop youth leaders who respond to disrespect with value and respect, and who focus on the positive wherever possible. Doing so involves digging deep, tapping into the good inside to respond with calm respect.

In football, if someone is on the receiving end of a bad tackle and the referee doesn't call it, it's appropriate to talk to the other player, to let him know that the tackle wasn't legal, but it must be done respectfully, not with cursing and verbal abuse. That conversation might go something like this: "Hey, man, that's a bad tackle. Come on. You can do better, all right? Let's have a good game."

This is the kind of conversation we want to facilitate with young people; we want them to see that it's possible to point out something inappropriate or unacceptable without being disrespectful. It's not appropriate to get in someone's face and say, "Hey, what the hell is wrong with you? What kind of tackle was that?" We also want to show young people that if they're confronted in this way, it's best to turn away rather than respond with disrespect.

The hard part is valuing another person even though he

did something inappropriate. We want youth leaders to not only respect the individual who acted unacceptably but also value him—that is, tap into the good inside. A conversation that points out the error but also expresses value might go like this: "Man, you were running really fast, but that tackle was a little too hard, OK? Let's go." Situations like this will most likely arise in our youth programs, so we have opportunities to model these respectful conversations in an authentic setting.

PERCEPTION AND AWARENESS

Communication involves perception—both of ourselves and others. To communicate effectively, we must be aware of how we see ourselves and how we view others. We must also understand how our thoughts and the thoughts of others influence our actions. Considering perception and awareness in communication enables us to behave in a way that is true to who we really want to be and to let others do the same.

Communication occurs between people, not inanimate objects. Each person has unique interests and mind-sets and ways of viewing the world. Understanding these will enable us to have deeper, more meaningful conversations.

We use a lineup activity to illustrate this idea of perception and awareness. We have people line up based on a skill they think they have. For example, we pick a skill such as cooking and say, "Line up according to your cooking skill level. Excellent skill level starts at the far left and goes down to poor at the far right." Everyone has to decide where they fit in the line, from excellent to poor. After everyone lines up, we pick another skill, say, singing, and let people move according to where they fit, from excellent to poor.

Then we move into more sensitive or controversial topics, things such as leadership skills, ethnicity, and religion. Sometimes we ask people to line up on the basis of spirituality: "Do you see yourself as spiritual or nonspiritual?" Some people consider themselves spiritual, but they don't go to church; they don't want to be associated with a formal church group, but they want to be associated with spirituality and prayerfulness. Other people consider spirituality inextricably linked to church—that is, you can't be spiritual without going to church. Beliefs on that spiritual–not spiritual continuum can generate heated conversations. For example, if participant A lines up on the highly spiritual end, participant B might question her friend's position based on what she knows about participant A—she doesn't go to church, she doesn't believe in organized religion, or whatever.

With the more sensitive topics in particular, it's interesting to watch people hesitate as they move. They're looking to see what other people are doing, and they're also thinking about what people are thinking about them. They might be thinking, *If I put myself at the top of the leadership line, what will people think? Will they think I'm boasting?* Or on the other end: *If I put myself down at the poor end of the leadership line, will people see me as humble, or will they see me as weak?*

The understanding part comes when participants explain why they stand where they do in line. In a situation where people know one another, they might be surprised when someone lines up at the spiritual end of the line, when most people in the group thought of her as not spiritual. When asked why she's at that end, the person might say, "I'm down on this end because even though I don't go to church, I'm a very spiritual person. And this is what I do and this is what I believe." People in the group may have never had the chance to have a conversation about spiritual things with this person, but now they understand her in a new way. The opportunity for communication gave the individual a safe space to share and gave the others a chance to listen, appreciate, and value who the individual is based on her line position and explanation.

One of the lineup pairs I find most intriguing is leader-follower. When I do this activity, I watch who goes to the leader end and who goes to the follower end of the line. Often, someone I thought of as a leader stands at the follower end. When we have a conversation about why he moved to the follower end, he might say something like, "Yes, I am a leader, but I'm more of a team player than a leader." The conversation helps others in the room, too, because maybe they haven't considered where team players fit on the continuum or maybe that understanding influences where they stand on the line. The discussion helps people understand themselves and each other in that context.

The goal of this learning experience is to illustrate that perception—both self-perception and perception of others—is the starting point of communication. After people line up, we lead a reflection activity. When we start with the first few skills—good dancer or not-so-good dancer, highly skilled dribbler or not so skilled, or whatever—the conversations are not too serious. But when we move into more sensitive topics—for example, dark skin or light skin, leader or follower, strong or weak—the discussions become more serious, and it relates to perceptions. We might start the dialogue with an open-ended question such as, "Does anyone want to share an observation?" If no one responds, we might get more specific: "So why did you choose to go to the top of this line?" And the person might respond, "Because I think I'm the best leader here." And then other people start jumping into the conversation. As the discussion unfolds, they learn what other people think about themselves and about others, and such understanding is a key part of communication.

As mentioned in the earlier chapters about designing learning experiences, we start with a challenge—in this case, picking a place in line. Then we have a conversation to debrief and reflect on what happened during the challenge. In this case, the reflection leads to an appreciation of self-perception and perception of others and the fact that people make decisions about where to stand based on what they think about themselves and what they think others are thinking.

In this activity, there is a lot of communication, both perceived and vocalized, that causes participants to do things and be things. The same thing happens in schools—children act and interact in certain ways. It's sometimes called peer pressure, but it might also be peer involvement and peer perception. Children might think, *I'm going to do this because I want people to think this is who I am.*

This aspect of communication relates to leadership because leadership involves understanding where each person is coming from; to make decisions as a group, leaders must understand themselves and others, and this happens through communication.

MECHANICS

The mechanics of communication involve how we say what we say. We sometimes call it the operational side of communication—the ways in which we share information so that our communication is clear, accurate, and effective. When leaders communicate, they cater to the learning styles of their teammates and use a variety of formats (verbal, visual, etc.) to ensure everyone understands. Leaders also make sure they have a clear purpose to their communication and that they provide useful, practical, accurate information. Communication is operationally or mechanically successful when the listener understands the speaker's message, intent, purpose, and so on.

Accuracy

Accuracy is especially important in certain types of communication—news, for example. When we talk about accuracy in relation to communication, we're not talking about personality or interpersonal relationships. We're talking about mechanics: the tactics we use to make sure our communication is correct, true, honest, and so forth.

Leaders ensure that they're making decisions based on accurate information coming to them. At the same time, they want to ensure that they are providing accurate information to others, whether it's members of the team, partner organizations, or the general public. Sending out inaccurate information not only causes challenges to those who receive it, but it can potentially weaken the leader's credibility. Leaders, therefore, have three key responsibilities in the context of accuracy:

1. To ensure that what they send out is accurate. This means double-checking with proper sources, reviewing, and so on before sending out messages. It is useful to have conversations to clarify or to send out drafts to team members for comments/review, before sending a final communication.
2. To verify accuracy of info before taking any actions. Unfortunately, we are bombarded with a significant amount of false and misleading info; leaders have a responsibility to sift out the truth.
3. To be honest—no pretending. Leaders often feel pressured to respond to requests for info and to make up information to avoid being embarrassed. Good leaders must recognize that there are many times when they may not have the answers. In those circumstances, the leader's responsibility is to acknowledge that she doesn't know, in which case, she has the option to delegate to another teammate who may be better placed to respond or to take action.

Purpose

Purpose relates to why people have a conversation. People communicate for many different reasons; sometimes we need to talk to someone to clear up an issue or get a better understanding of what someone is thinking about a certain topic. Purpose determines tone of voice, type of questions, and other operational aspects of communication. For example, if we're having a conversation to clarify an issue, we won't challenge someone with pointed questions; instead, we'll speak in comforting tones. Understanding the purpose behind communication helps to facilitate the conversation.

COMMUNICATION WITH INDIVIDUALS AND GROUPS

Communication involves people, and the number of people involved in a conversation influences how we communicate. The group dynamic, for example, is often different than the one-on-one dynamic; we more readily drop our guard in one-on-one situations and feel comfortable sharing on a personal level.

Our responsibility as coaches and teachers is to give young people opportunities to have meaningful conversations in both settings because both have value. In one-on-one situations, both participants have to talk; individuals who are naturally quiet might be able to hide in group settings, but this isn't an option when they're talking with just one other person. At the same time, however, there's a richness that comes out of a group conversation. A young person might hear someone share an idea that he was thinking about, and this might give him the courage to add on to the first person's comment.

In working with young people, context and purpose determine the type of communication we encourage. We may have participants choose their partners or groups; this usually makes them feel more comfortable, but it may not always be the better option. Sometimes, we place young people in pairs or groups with people who are less likely to come together naturally. This will probably produce an entirely different outcome. Sometimes, we use a blind selection method, so the pairing is completely random. It all depends on context.

No matter which communication style we set up, we have a responsibility to create a comfortable environment for sharing, one that builds trust and facilitates openness.

FACILITATING GOOD COMMUNICATION SKILLS

In addition to the activities mentioned, we use several learning experiences to facilitate the awakening of communication skills, as well as an increased awareness of their value. These experiences often center on the idea of using limitations.

Sometimes we blindfold the whole group and ask them to perform a task; other times we leave one person without a blindfold. Or we might limit participants' ability to speak, or limit the use of their hands or legs, or use a gradual combination of limitations; it depends on the group and the intended outcomes.

The blindfolded experiences tend to be the most challenging. They may take the form of a modified team sport; for example, while wearing blindfolds, participants must pass around a basketball to get it from one end of the court to the other. Players soon work out that it's easier to use a bounce pass than a chest pass because the sound of the bounce helps the receiver to gauge the direction of the pass. They also use lots of verbal communication to assess the location of teammates and to ensure that receivers are ready to receive before passers make a pass. Limitations such as blindfolds help the participants become more aware of their other senses, whether it's sound or touch; they also make participants more acutely focused on the need and value of good communication in completing a team task.

I like to ask questions to get groups thinking about the value of communication. A couple of these questions come from conversations I've had with a Master Artist from Trinidad, who first appeared to me as very intimidating, with a formidable look in his eyes and a powerful, mighty voice to match his stature. But I discovered that when he lets you into his thinking space, he's wise beyond words and deeply thoughtful about life. He asked me once, "If you had a hundred words left to speak, what would you say?" Another time he asked, "If you had only one hundred steps left, where would you go? Where would you walk?"

When we pose questions such as these, we get young people thinking about the value of words and how we use them, and the value of where we go and how we use our time. This is an important consideration in the context of communication. When we impose limitations on communication and then have conversations around those limitations, we see the power of communication and the importance of choosing one's words wisely. It helps us understand what's important in what we communicate and how we communicate.

Communication games such as Whisper Down the Lane or Telephone are simple experiences that can be used to illustrate the importance of accurate information. The game starts with the first person whispering a sentence to the next person, who then whispers it to the next person, and so on. At the end, the last person repeats the sentence out loud, and usually, it's quite different from the original sentence. This game involves limitations because each person knows only what the person before has told them.

Solid communication is a foundation for good leadership.

When we provide experiences like these, in both sport and nonsport settings, we help young people see the value of good communication and give them opportunities to practice a skill they will use for life.

> **FOR REFLECTION**
>
> 1. Respectful communication is the basis of relationship building. As we openly and honestly exchange information, we develop transparency and trust—two key parts of communication in leadership.
>
> 2. Consider your own communication skills. What past experiences have contributed to the development of this leadership skill in you? How have you been using sport to develop communication skills in young people?
>
> 3. What new ideas about communication did this chapter awaken, and how can you apply these to facilitate youth leadership development in your sport setting?

CHAPTER 6

Teamwork

Young people need teamwork skills, whether they're playing basketball, finishing a group science project, or working with siblings on a gift for Dad. Regardless of someone's specific role within a team, successful teamwork rests on several key qualities that every young person can learn—trust, commitment, and accountability in particular. This chapter covers the basis of good teamwork and what leading a team looks like, as well as learning experiences you can use to facilitate the awakening of this skill.

THE BASIS OF GOOD TEAMWORK

When I lectured at the Teacher's College, one of my colleagues brought in a guest speaker to talk about relationships. He was a guru-looking kind of guy; he had long hair and white cotton clothing, and he was wearing leather sandals. I was a little nervous at first because my relatively young student-teachers were often impatient, with a preference for short, interactive lectures. As the guest lecturer approached the lecture hall, I could see the expressions of concern on the faces of the student-teachers—this was not looking like it was going to be very exciting. Fortunately, it turned out to be both inspiring and entertaining and provided yet another lesson about perceptions.

The guest lecturer told the young student-teachers, "Relationships are really tricky. Let's say I tell you ten things about yourself, and nine of them are good things. I see your beautiful eyes, I love your personality, you communicate very well, and so on. Then I tell you one negative thing—your nose is kind of big. I've told you ten things about yourself; nine are good and only one is bad. You won't even remember the good things. You'll remember only the bad. In fact, you'll not only remember; you'll hold it against me and you'll say, 'Well, who is this man with ugly long hair telling me that I have a big nose?'"

He went on: "Before I tell you anything about yourself, good or bad, it's really important that we have a relationship." This struck me because of my position at the Teacher's College and the emphasis on building relationships with student-teachers—professionally intimate relationships. Before a lecturer can critique a beginning teacher's style or presentation, the two must have a relationship; otherwise, the student-teacher may not receive the criticism in the helpful spirit in which it is given. The relationship should be not only professional but also intimate, which is why I use the term *professionally intimate*.

If we are going to be part of a team—whether it's a project team or sports team—we need to get to know people intimately and build relationships. Relationships are the core of teamwork, and building those relationships requires respectful communication and an awareness of the perceptions of both ourselves and others.

As mentioned earlier, every person on a team—no matter what kind of team—plays a role. Each team usually has a team captain or leader, but there are many other roles, and each team member has the opportunity to use leadership skills in his or her role.

LEADING A TEAM

Leading a team involves four interrelated components. As teachers and coaches, we need to first practice these skills ourselves; through the learning experiences we create, we can then facilitate awakening and practice among young people:

1. *Remember, we're leading people and not objects.* Leading

footballs would be easy; they don't have thoughts, feelings, opinions, and so on. Because we're leading people, we need to...

2. *Develop meaningful relationships.* As we develop meaningful relationships, we come to understand and appreciate those we're leading. As discussed, communication is a key part of relationship building; therefore, to lead a team we should...

3. *Learn to communicate clearly and effectively.* As we listen to others and share information respectfully and effectively, we gain the trust of those on our team. Within the context of the team and within any given relationship, there will be various levels. Therefore, we need to...

4. *Understand the different levels of relationship.* In any relationship—even a close one—there are things that remain unspoken, whether because they would be offensive or because the relationship is still new and the information is too personal. It's important to understand what we can do and say in any given relationship.

LEVELS OF RELATIONSHIP

When we build a team and relationships with the members of that team, we use intuition to understand where we are in each relationship—that is, what we can say, how to say it, and so on. Understanding the different relationship levels, we might present the same information in different ways to different people; we might reframe the question or comment so that it matches the level of our relationship. Even at the strongest, most solid relationship level, there are still issues we should address carefully. Ultimately, we want to get to the place where we are at the highest level with each team member, where we value each person's contribution even if we don't agree with or understand their position.

The levels of relationship can be thought of in the same way as Hellison's levels of personal and social responsibility referenced in the first section of the book. We might start at the lowest level of "I don't really care what you think" and then move up to tolerating: "I don't agree with what you're saying, but I can tolerate it." Tolerating is OK. Then we might move up to the next level: "Even though I don't fully understand what you're saying, I'm not just tolerating it; because of the level of our relationship, I am now valuing your point of view." When we move to this level, the team as a whole improves because we're valuing and, therefore, more open to incorporating the contribution of all team members.

To facilitate the development of teamwork and high-level relationships, we need to create learning experiences for young people that challenge their relationship value. For example, you could have the team work on a task and then at some point in the middle or at the end, start a conversation about relationships. This conversation could be facilitated by the adult or by the group or in pairs. The key as a facilitator is to give young people a challenge that provides an opportunity to engage in a situation that creates misunderstanding, frustration, or some other point of conflict in their relationship. Then we observe the team as they work through the situation and allow them to reflect on the experience.

WAYS TO FACILITATE TEAMWORK

Many team challenges in both sport and nonsport settings can be used as appropriate learning experiences to facilitate a deeper understanding of the value of relationships—from building straw towers and paper bridges to solving puzzles and strategizing in small-sided basketball, football, or volleyball games. The key element in designing the learning experience is to provide a challenge that potentially confronts the relationships between and among teammates. In small-sided games, these learning experiences are further enhanced with the use of uneven teams (e.g., three versus five possession football).

When we give teams the task of designing and building the tallest tower using straws and tape, we often see a variety of designs and an equal amount of failure and success. This simple learning experience challenges teammates to work together, and we've found that the most successful teams are the ones that value the contributions of all teammates. The least successful teams are those where some team members are dominating the tasks, while others are only minimally engaged.

Another learning experience you can use is building a puzzle. Give each team member some of the puzzle pieces and ask them all to work as a team to complete the puzzle. You may add limitations; for example, tell participants they are not allowed to touch the pieces from other teammates and/or they are not allowed to speak during the task. Then you can manipulate the experience to create the challenge. For example, you could give each person the same number of pieces and also keep a few pieces hidden so that the team is unable to successfully complete the puzzle. Participants think all of the pieces are there; they don't know you have engineered the environment to create a situation for potential conflict. In that setting, people will have different ideas on how to proceed. Someone will probably not want to work with someone else because that's human nature. Some people like big pictures, some people like small pictures, some people like to work in compartments—the situation will potentially lead to conflict.

During the experience or at the end of it, the coach facilitates reflection on the key content. In this case, we want to awaken an understanding about relationships. So you might start with a self-reflection and then move into pair or group discussion. For example, you might say, "I want you to think about how that activity went and specifically to reflect on the process and interactions between and among members of the group," and then have the participants write down their answers individually; that's the self-reflection. If you choose to do peer reflections, you may then invite participants to have a conversation in pairs—essentially sharing their personal reflections. Before participants pair up, it may be useful to give them some guidelines about good listening, seeking clarification, and being nonjudgmental. This helps to create a safe environment for the one-on-one conversation; it allows individuals to share their personal thoughts and to explain their observations.

At the end, you bring the group together and facilitate a debriefing. You might ask, "What are the key things we learned from this experience?" and let the young people share their thoughts.

As facilitators, we want to ask questions that help young people identify where they are, where they want to be, and how they can get there. In terms of teamwork, these conversations lead to better understanding of the individual team members and how we can all work better as a team.

For example, through these conversations, the team leader may realize that one team member, Susan, likes to talk. At first, the leader may tolerate Susan's talkative nature, but the goal is to move to the next level and value Susan's contribution. When the leader moves on to valuing, she might give Susan more opportunities to talk. When this happens, the whole team benefits because Susan, and every other team member, is being given an opportunity to contribute in his or her own way.

> **FOR REFLECTION**
>
> 1. Teamwork is founded on relationships. Leaders learn to value the contribution of individual team members and learn from each person, which ultimately builds a stronger team.
>
> 2. Consider your own teamwork skills. What past experiences have contributed to the development of this leadership skill in you? How have you been using sport to develop teamwork skills in young people?
>
> 3. What new ideas about teamwork did this chapter awaken, and how can you apply these to facilitate youth leadership development in your sport setting?

CHAPTER 7

Resourcefulness

Resourcefulness is the ability to successfully cope with new or difficult situations. It involves being solution oriented—looking for solutions to challenges based on what you have, even if those resources are minimal.

When I was in scouts growing up, we often had no choice but to be resourceful. At camp, for example, leaders gave us tasks with limited supplies. Sometimes we rowed out into the bay to fish, but we had only a short piece of fishing line and one hook—no fancy rod and no bait. As a team, we had to decide what to use as bait and how to fish without a rod. When we came back, we didn't have pots and pans, so we had to decide how to prepare the meal.

Likewise, in the context of sport, we can create challenges that awaken resourcefulness in young people—both in terms of the leadership skill itself and the sports skill being used.

WHAT DOES RESOURCEFULNESS INVOLVE?

Resourcefulness has two main components: defining what is possible and adding value.

1. DEFINING THE POSSIBLE
Be Open to New Possibilities

The sport and scouting settings both have many opportunities to awaken resourcefulness. In the preceding scouting scenario, for example, the goal is to awaken resourcefulness without saying, "You need to be resourceful. Go fish without bait." Scouts learn the skill in the context of the challenge; they have to be resourceful to catch the fish.

The same applies in a sport context. We create learning experiences that challenge young people to use resourcefulness, but we don't tell them to be resourceful. At the end of the experience, young people figure out that in order to be resourceful, they need to be open to new possibilities. For example, we might create a challenge that involves finding team sponsorship. To complete the task, young people must first ask themselves, "What are the possibilities?" The possibilities may involve partnering with a city council or writing letters to corporate sponsors. Knowing there are options is the starting point for resourcefulness; in other words, we must believe there are possibilities for solving the challenge before we can be resourceful. Belief leads to achievement.

If young people don't believe they can solve a challenge—if they don't see the options or are not open to possibilities—they are not going to solve it. In the sports realm, a team might look at the opponent and think, *Look how tall these guys are. How are we going to pass around them? How are we going to score?* With that mind-set, they will not win. But if the team believes there are options, they can be resourceful and meet the challenge.

The 1970s Chinese men's volleyball team provides a perfect example. The traditional volleyball game involves a pass to the setter, who puts the ball up high near the net for the spiker to hit it over. However, the Chinese players were shorter than the European players; they couldn't compete in this traditional high, outside set-hit play because the Europeans could easily anticipate and block the hits from their shorter opponents. So the Chinese looked for options to compensate for their lack of height. They came up with a short, quick set to the middle rather than a high ball to the outside. The Chinese didn't say, "We can't play this game. Let's try something else." They were open to possibilities, which led to resourcefulness.

Whether it's a school project, game situation, or life event, developing resourcefulness starts with believing there's a way to meet the challenge.

Adopt a Realistic Attitude

Defining what's possible also involves pragmatism. We want to encourage young people to believe a task is doable, to be open to possibilities, but also to know what's realistic given the specific situation. This is a key leadership skill: being able to balance belief in options and understanding what can actually be done.

For example, if we're organizing a local 5K race, we want to first be open to possibilities regarding how to attract participants. This means approaching the challenge with a "Yes, we can" attitude rather than "No one likes to run. How are we going to get participants?" In addition, we need to know our limits—we probably can't get ten thousand people to run in our local 5K, but we might be able to attract five hundred; that is a realistic goal. A good leader can also help her team adopt this balanced perspective.

Anticipate Likely Challenges

Defining what's possible also involves anticipating challenges and being prepared to meet complications that arise. To anticipate and prepare, we must look forward, think through the whole situation, and imagine what obstacles to success we might encounter. Then we can think through potential solutions—again, being open to possibilities—and apply them as appropriate. As facilitators, we work through this process with the learning experiences we design, but we also want to awaken this leadership skill in the young people engaged in the challenge. We can do this by having them brainstorm the key challenges that may arise for a particular situation and then have them identify possible solutions for each scenario. For example, if they are planning a 5K road race, they may identify challenges with online registration for runners who do not have Internet access. They may provide a solution that offers face-to-face registration on a particular day at a particular venue as one possible solution.

2. ADDING VALUE

In working with young people, we want to communicate that resourcefulness is more than just figuring out how to get by with what we have; it also entails adding value and making a situation or project better. Adding value involves innovation, leading by example, and doing more with less.

Be Innovative

Innovation has two parts: creating something brand new

or making an old process work better. In either case, we add value through our resourcefulness. For example, organizing a 5K is not a new idea, but we can consider ways to improve aspects of the usual format, prizes, and so on. Likewise, many volleyball teams now use the short, quick set style of play; our team might look for ways to improve that style to give us the edge.

As facilitators, we want to encourage young people to ask themselves, "What innovation can we add that will get us through this challenge (more) successfully?" With questions like this, we help youth see that resourcefulness is more than finding a solution and getting through a task; it is also about improving or adding value to a solution that already exists. Adding value in the context of resourcefulness is a key leadership skill.

WHY IS RESOURCEFULNESS IMPORTANT?

Awakening resourcefulness in young people helps them avoid paralysis in the face of challenges. In our society, many things are ready made and easily accessible. As a result, the need for daily resourcefulness is minimal. If students have a school project to develop, for example, they can often find a completed version online somewhere.

However, there are times when a solution is not readily available, and young people can become paralyzed because they don't know how to figure out what to do. By awakening resourcefulness in youth, we give them the tools they need to face life situations that don't have ready-made solutions. We want them to see they have options even when they don't immediately have what they need—matches to light a fire, a team full of tall players, materials to finish a project, and so on.

If young people don't see the possibilities, if they don't believe they can succeed, they will give up, and we don't want them to give up, whether it's on the playing field, on a school project, during an exam, in a relationship, or in any other life circumstance. We want young people to recognize that they always have options and that if they're open to these possibilities, they can make something happen. The extreme end of believing there are no options is suicidal thoughts. Ultimately, the goal of the learning experiences we create in our programs and on the playing field is awakening skills young people will use for a lifetime, and resourcefulness is key in terms of maintaining hope in life.

As facilitators, we can awaken resourcefulness and help young people avoid the cliff of paralysis through a strength-based approach. First, we want to awaken the ability to start with an open mind—that is, to be open to new possibilities for tackling the seemingly impossible challenge. Next, we want to help young people take stock of what they have. For example, a team might think through it this way: "OK, we don't have tall players like our opponent, but what do we have? We have Jimmy, who's really fast. We've got Mario, who's really witty. So maybe we can outsmart the other team using our speed and wits." This is a strengths-based approach—starting with the strengths you already have. Focusing on what we don't have leads to paralysis, but focusing on what we do have leads to a "We can do this" attitude.

HOW DO LEADERS DEMONSTRATE RESOURCEFULNESS?

The following qualities characterize a good leader, specifically in the area of resourcefulness. It's important to remember these qualities, or skills, can be learned—in the same way math or writing skills can be learned. The young people in your program or on your team may not currently demonstrate these qualities, but they have the capacity. Our responsibility as facilitators is to awaken these qualities through carefully designed learning experiences and opportunities for reflection.

ACCEPT RESPONSIBILITY

Leaders accept responsibility for accomplishing a task, even if they hit obstacles. Leaders believe there are options, they embrace those new possibilities, and they don't give up. Accepting responsibility engenders that can-do attitude. If we know that we are responsible for a certain task, we will look at what we have (strengths), we will be open to possibilities, and we will make it happen to the best of our ability. In short, a leader who accepts responsibility will use resourcefulness to make sure the task is completed. He or she will tap into the talents on the team—speed, common sense, agility, and so on—to get it done. Accepting responsibility doesn't mean the leader does it all; it means he or she makes sure the task gets done using the people and other resources available.

Whether someone is the leader of a scout patrol going to camp or football team facing a bigger team or group organizing a 5K, that person needs to first accept responsibility for accomplishing the task; resourcefulness will follow.

ASSESS THE SITUATION

Leaders have the ability to assess a situation in a realistic way—that is, they can look at the task to be completed, the resources available, the strengths on the team, and the potential for innovation and see the possible solutions based on these factors. Being a skilled assessor involves paying attention in a new situation, being aware of the resources and circumstances. As mentioned earlier, an effective leader/assessor can balance the belief that the task can be accomplished and an understanding of how it can be accomplished realistically.

ADDRESS THE CONDITIONS

Leaders operate skillfully and inventively to address the conditions in front of them. Sometimes, this requires an ability to assess the situation and quickly address the challenge. For example, if a team is getting beat up by the opponent, the leader needs to address this promptly and not let it continue. First, the leader must understand what the problem is: Is the defensive strategy not working? Does one of the defenders keep getting beat by the opposing striker? Then the leader can address the issue given the resource available—for example, switching to zone defense or making a player substitution to someone who is quicker.

It's human nature to drag our feet when we see a problem, but we don't think we have the resources to fix it. So we don't act and the situation deteriorates. As mentioned, a leader accepts responsibility for completing the task, and sometimes this involves acting quickly—not ignoring or waiting for the situation to correct itself. It also involves adept intervention: communicating with respect, using teamwork, and implementing other leadership skills addressed here.

CREATE ACCESS TO INFORMATION

Leaders know how to create access to information or resources when they are not immediately available. For example, a task might involve designing a team logo. The team meets, and the leader realizes no one has expertise in logo design—that skill or resource is not readily available. But the leader asks questions and discovers that someone has a brother who knows graphic design. The leader knows she is responsible for getting this logo designed and figures out a way to gain access to that resource. If the leader doesn't see the resource in the team, she knows to go outside the team—make a phone call, check online, whatever it takes to find the needed resource. Leaders are not limited by the resources in front of them; they look elsewhere if necessary. They think outside the box for other possibilities.

WAYS TO FACILITATE RESOURCEFULNESS

To awaken the skill of resourcefulness, we need to design learning experiences that involve a challenge—to build something, for example—and limit the resources with which to complete that challenge. The key is limiting the participants' resources: we want them to look at what they need to do—consider their available materials, their people skills, and so on—and then figure out how to make it happen with what they have.

The way in which facilitators limit resources depends on the goal of the experience. Sometimes we limit participants to what they physically have in front of them. In our youth programs, we use a task with newspaper and masking tape. We tell the group, "We're going to play a baseball-type game, but we don't have any equipment. All we have is this newspaper and masking tape." We don't tell them what to do—we don't tell them what equipment to make or how to make it—but they still come up with designs for a solid ball and bat. They use resourcefulness because the challenge requires it. At the end of the activity, we debrief and bring out the fact that the young people showed resourcefulness: they accepted responsibility for making the game happen, they were open to possibilities, they looked at what they had, they innovated, and they came up with a solution.

Other times, you might give participants a challenge and let them use an extended network; in other words, what they have includes the physical resources in front of them as well as the people they can call, the websites they can search, and so on. In our youth programs, we use a learning experience that involves figuring out what to use for prizes at the end of a tournament. The scenario is this: The organizing committee originally had a budget of $4,000 for prizes, but most of the money was spent on other things. Now they have only $300. What can they do for prizes with what they have? The group has to brainstorm ideas, and they can use outside resources to get the prizes. They might decide to use chocolate or fruit; now they have to figure out how to get to the store and buy these items.

Our role as facilitator starts with designing an experience that brings out the desired response in the young people—in this case resourcefulness, but it also might be a specific aspect of resourcefulness. We create a challenge by limiting the available resources. Sometimes we might be very literal; we might not even ask participants what they have but instead tell them outright, "This is what you have, and this is what you need to do."

Our role continues as we monitor the experiences and the participants' involvement in them. Specifically, we evaluate whether the challenge has the correct level of difficulty and whether young people are indeed using resourcefulness as intended.

For example, we might throw in a challenge like this: "In your team of six, you have to design your own football goals for this small-goal tournament, and you have these resources to work with. You have forty minutes to create the design. Remember, you can do this, but you cannot do that. Any questions?" While the groups work, we walk around and observe. We're looking to see if any group is struggling, or if everyone is finding the task too easy. In doing so, we're using the diagnostic-prescriptive approach discussed earlier: we're finding out what the participants need, and we're making modifications to meet that need. As facilitators, we must intervene if the experience is not producing the desired results. We might just need to ask a few questions to get the group thinking in a different direction—for example, "What do you have? Is there another way you could use that? How could you use this piece?"

Facilitating is part art, part science; it's knowing your group of kids and knowing how to nudge them toward understanding without telling them outright.

> ### FOR REFLECTION
>
> 1. Resourcefulness should not only be viewed in terms of making the best of limited resources. It also involves innovation and adding value to something that already exists.
>
> 2. Consider your own resourcefulness. What past experiences have contributed to the development of this leadership skill in you? How have you been using sport to develop resourcefulness in young people?
>
> 3. What new ideas about resourcefulness did this chapter awaken, and how can you apply these to facilitate youth leadership development in your sport setting?

CHAPTER 8

Adaptability

In the CSDA model, we define adaptability as the capacity to readily adjust oneself to different conditions. Adaptability and resourcefulness are closely related; in fact, all of the leadership skills presented in this book intertwine. However, adaptability is not necessarily about being resourceful; it involves a pragmatic willingness to adjust and change strategy based on the given circumstances and resources.

Leaders must be willing to adapt. Even if adapting makes a leader uncomfortable, he or she must be committed to making the necessary changes. Leaders, myself included, tend to have a particular way of doing things, and we usually don't change our style until we encounter a challenge or missing resource that forces us to do so. Instead, we should be open to changing, whether because there's a missing resource or because it's a team decision or because it will create a different result for the program. In this sense, adaptability entails a willingness to operate outside one's comfort zone.

Adaptability also involves learning continuously. Leaders should not be stuck in one particular mode of operation but instead be open to learning new ways of doing things. This is especially true for people who lead teams of people who are younger or older or somehow different from themselves. I had a young team at the office, and they frequently came up with crazy ideas. I often thought my way was better and had to learn to adapt to their new ideas and new ways of doing things.

One example is flexitime. I loved being the first one at the office. Our office location is in close proximity to Quinam Bay, and some mornings I would get there very early, go for a run along Quinam Beach just as the sun came up, take a swim, and then head to the office, where I would shower, change, eat breakfast, and have a quiet space for about an hour before others arrived. I enjoyed being there early so I could greet staff when they arrived. I liked being able to chat with coworkers over lunch and then say goodbye when they left at the end of the day.

Flexitime changed this dynamic, and it took me a while to adapt. With the flexitime arrangement, staff didn't come in to the office every day—only if the task demanded it. I work from home a lot now, too, and we no longer have full-time staff at the office. The reality is that people don't need to be in the office to get their work done, but it has been challenging for me to adjust to this new work environment that doesn't involve clocking in and having everyone together. As a leader, I've had to learn to adapt to environmental and cultural changes.

As leaders, we want things to happen and to happen successfully; we don't just want to maintain the status quo or usual way of doing something. It's important to ask ourselves, "Is the way we're doing things fulfilling the intended purpose? Is it doing so in the best way possible?" The bottom line is whether the method is meeting the intended outcome, not whether we're doing something in a particular way. Clocking in from eight to four or conducting workshops using a particular template or keeping the name of a certain project—these things are not the end goal; the end goal is successfully completed projects and workshops that produce the desired outcome for those who attend.

A personal example: In the very early days of CSDA, we developed a program based on fundamental motor skills and modified sport that we implemented as both an in-school (physical education) and an after-school program. In the beginning, we branded the program as the

Youth Sport Program, and then some time later, because of a partnership with the International Alliance for Youth Sport (IAYS), we rebranded the program as GameOn.

After the partnership with IAYS had expired, we decided to rename the program. Some of the new (young) staff who were delivering the program came up with ENGAGE360 as the new name for the program, and for some reason, it just didn't resonate with me. But the young staff did an excellent job of justifying the change and capturing the reasoning behind the new brand. Initially, maybe because of the years I spent working on the program as GameOn, I struggled with the new name, but I needed to be open to this change; eventually, I embraced it based on the suggestions of the young staff.

Sometimes it's a challenge to let go of processes we've set up and projects we've created because it feels like we're losing something. But a leader must adapt to the reality in front of him or her. In my case, the young people were taking the organization in a new, more current direction, and I had to be pragmatic and adjust.

WHAT DOES ADAPTATION INVOLVE?

In general, adaptation is a process and not an instantaneous event. Adapting to a new idea, policy, or procedure happens gradually, in stages, as a person goes through mental and emotional shifts to adjust to the new situation and take a different action. The process includes three elements:

1. Mental shift. When faced with a situation that requires adaptability, young leaders need to adjust their thinking to address the particular circumstances in front of them. They need to shift from seeing a problem to seeing new possibilities and opportunities.
2. Emotional reframing. Similarly, when faced with situations that require adaptability, young leaders must reframe their emotions: from negative, fearful, and frustrated to positive, agreeable, and confident.
3. Commitment to new action. Ultimately, when faced with situations that require adaptability, young leaders need to adjust their actions; they must head in a different direction as dictated by the new circumstances.

As people work through the process of adapting in mind, emotion, and action, they accomplish two of the overarching principles of adaption: adjusting to change and being flexible.

ADJUSTING TO CHANGE

Adapting is more than just accepting; leaders need to embrace the change and be an advocate for it, because the leaders' response to change affects the whole team—it sets the example. As with other skills we've discussed, there are different levels of adapting: at the lowest level, we are open to knowing and understanding the new idea; at the next level, we begin to accept it; and at the highest level, we move to valuing the change. When we reach the highest level of valuing, we embrace the change and advocate for it; if you're on a team, all members need to be in the same place of owning the change and believing in it. If everyone is not on board, the team is weakened, as is the entire project or brand. Adaptation does not mean giving in and saying OK; it involves commitment to the change in a meaningful and tangible way.

In my earlier example of changing the project name from GameOn to ENGAGE360, I did not easily progress to valuing. My team really had to push and share the justification behind the change. In this way, communication played a role; we discussed the change and what it would mean for future projects and decisions. As the young team members shared their ideas and we had a conversation, I came to see their point of view and eventually to value it.

Communication also plays a role in explaining to newcomers and people outside the organization *why* the change is being made—the purpose. Leaders don't decide to make a change just because they feel like making a change; leaders make changes because they've thought through the options, and it makes sense to move in this direction.

Leaders help their team adjust when they communicate what is being changed and why. As people adapt, they truly embrace the change and use it as an opportunity to grow and learn; it's a continual process, one that we want to communicate to the young people in our leadership programs.

People work more effectively when they understand why changes are being made; they adapt more readily when they understand why they're adapting. When we understand, we adjust our priorities based on the change, which helps us to better deal with whatever those changes are.

The goal is to facilitate this adaptability on a metalevel with young people on our teams and in our programs. In other words, if change is coming, communicate it to the group so they see how a leader (you) handles change; how a leader adapts, adjusts, and embraces the new situation; and how a leader communicates change to others on the team.

If you are a coach, for example, you might say to your team, "We're moving our training to a venue that's a little farther away because we no longer have access to the washrooms at this facility," or "We're not going to do any jump serves today, as I want you to focus on accuracy/placement rather than power." Whenever there is a need to adapt, communication is important so that all team members understand the reason for the change and, even better, can participate in the conversation leading up to it. This, in turn, makes for a less ambiguous climate in which everyone understands the modification, embraces it, and advocates for it, which in turn leads to a stronger, more effective team because everyone believes in change they're participating in. The whole team sees the bigger picture.

BEING FLEXIBLE

Adaptability necessarily involves being flexible, and flexibility entails compromise, although not in the sense of compromising on principles. Sometimes in order to achieve the desired end result, we have to give in on something. It's not a loss; it's a strategic way of getting to the goal. In leadership, there's a give-and-take based on achieving the final purpose.

Being flexible in a sport setting might look like this: Let's say two teams show up at the same time to use a basketball court for practice. One coach decides to let the other team use it, even though he thinks his team signed up for the space first. The coach should not go back to his team and act as though they lost. Instead, he could say, "Today, we gave the other team the opportunity to practice, but that gives us the chance to work on speed and agility using the outdoor training field." As coaches, we model this positive spin—we are being flexible, adapting to the situation, and also seeing how we can turn it into something beneficial: a chance to work on other things.

HOW DO LEADERS DEMONSTRATE ADAPTABILITY?

Leaders can model adaptability in many ways. Here are just three:

1. Respond positively. Regardless of the situation, leaders demonstrate adaptability by controlling their emotions so that they don't react negatively.
2. Be creative (but not reckless). Whatever the challenge, leaders brainstorm multiple solutions and ideas and think through the likely outcomes. If possible, they test options before taking action.
3. Be informed. Leaders don't limit themselves to the information they have at hand. Instead, they seek new ideas, facts, and material from a variety of sources to enhance their response to the situation.

WAYS TO FACILITATE ADAPTABILITY

In our programs with young people, we use several experiences to bring out adaptability as well as resourcefulness. One such experience involves designing a game with certain limitations: space, time, equipment, numbers of people, and so on. We give participants ten minutes to design a game; the game must have the playing space outlined, a certain number of rules (sometimes we say no more than five rules), a name, and so on. Participants design a game on their own first, and then they pair up; the two young people discuss their respective games and come up with a single game out of their two. This discussion involves negotiation, communication, and adaptability.

After ten minutes, the pairs have to present the game they have created out of the two individual games. When we debrief at the end of this challenge, we might first ask questions to help them reflect on the experience in general—for example, "What did you gain from this experience? How could you have done this differently? What positive lesson came out of this? Did you feel this compromise was a setback? How so?" Then we might ask questions related to the skill of adaptability and, specifically, the mental, emotional, and action elements of the adaptation process—for example, "How did you respond mentally to the ideas of your colleagues? How did you feel (pleased, excited, indifferent) about your colleagues' design? Did you demonstrate a willingness to be open to new ideas, to be flexible, to compromise?" After this reflection, we have two pairs come together, so now participants A and B have to negotiate with participants C and D to come up with one game that follows the same original guidelines.

In addition to the leadership skill of adaptability/flexibility, this learning experience has the potential to facilitate the awakening of life skills such as respect and conflict resolution. Through the reflective discussions, we awaken young people's appreciation and understanding of the value of controlling emotions in the face of difficulties, being creative and committed to solving challenges, and remaining positive and open to exploring new opportunities.

One of the most challenging learning experiences that we use to facilitate adaptability among young people is the construction swap. We give each small group (or team) a bag of materials and a task—something to build. What's inside the bag varies according to the task, but each team receives the same materials. In one such task, team members must design and build a goal that they will use in a small-sided football tournament. Working as a team to complete this task has its inherent challenges that draw on several skills already discussed, including communication and resourcefulness.

After teams have completed their designs and have started building their goals, we stop the task and instruct teams to swap their incomplete projects—so each group is now working to complete another group's project—and we observe how they respond. Depending on time constraints, we may allow the teams to complete the task, or we may stop the challenge soon after the swap and engage the young people in a reflection exercise. We might ask, "How did you respond to the idea of having to give up your project to another team? How did you feel about having to take over a project that did not belong to you? What did you do to complete the challenge successfully?"

Many possible learning experiences can be designed to facilitate an awakening of adaptability. The key is to make sure the experience is challenging and that it requires participants to make adjustments at some point. The real value in the learning experience is the reflection and conversation—to get participants thinking individually, in partners, and as a whole group about their responses to the challenges. As already stated, we learn best by doing when we reflect on what we do.

> **FOR REFLECTION**
>
> 1. Adaptability enables leaders to overcome challenges. It is not a compromise of principles but an ability to adjust to changing situations.
>
> 2. Consider your own adaptability skills. What past experiences have contributed to the development of this leadership skill in you? How have you been using sport to develop adaptability in young people?
>
> 3. What new ideas about adaptability did this chapter awaken, and how can you apply these to facilitate youth leadership development in your sport setting?

CHAPTER 9

Delegation

Leaders are responsible for getting things done—not necessarily doing the thing itself but using whatever resources are available to successfully complete the task. Delegation is one of the main leadership skills involved in executing this responsibility.

With young people, it's important to make sure they understand that delegation does not mean shirking one's responsibilities or passing off the less desirable jobs to someone else. Instead, it's about identifying the resources you have—specifically, the human resources—that are best suited to effectively and efficiently complete certain tasks; it's about matching skill sets with tasks. A leader might delegate the job of getting the field lined, which in itself maybe be considered a leadership task different from actually lining the field. If someone is responsible for getting the field lined, he or she might delegate the manual lining to someone with the skills to do so.

When working with young people to develop delegation skills, we create teams or committees who are responsible for completing tasks that have been delegated to them. For example, we might assign the task of organizing the tournament's closing ceremony to Jonathan and his team. Then Jonathan has the opportunity to delegate different aspects of the closing ceremony to various team members; in this way, there's a division of roles based on each person's skill set and capacity and an opportunity for all members of the team to contribute meaningfully to the final product.

We might give Jonathan some guidelines as he delegates. For example, we might say that the closing ceremony events cannot run longer than one hour and that the guest speaker should be a representative from the sport community. Beyond that, Jonathan has the power of choice—he decides who performs each task. We also want to ensure all of the various tasks are meaningful and not menial so that each person feels entrusted with the responsibility to do something significant, something that involves making choices. This is a core part of the youth leadership development program: we always want to give young people choices. True leadership involves making decisions and, specifically, about meaningful, important things.

The overall goal in any project is completing it with efficiency and effectiveness. Common sense suggests that the leader can't do everything, so that person needs to develop an appreciation for the talents and skill sets of others on his or her team and delegate responsibilities as appropriate.

WHAT DOES DELEGATION INVOLVE?
ASSIGNMENT OF DUTIES

Assigning duties involves three steps:

1. Clearly define the task and the expected result.
2. Explain the task's purpose, including where it fits in the overall scheme of things.
3. Explain why the task is being delegated.

To facilitate an awakening of delegation skills, we give young people a challenge—for example, the overall task and duties to be delegated—but we don't spell out these three steps of successfully assigning duties. After the challenge is complete, we debrief, and without much prompting, the young people can usually tell us what needs to be done to make delegation successful. They can tell us it involves clearly defining the tasks, explaining the purpose, and explaining why the responsibility is being delegated. We often hear things such as, "Well, because my team leader was really clear about what she wanted me to do and what the expected results should be, I understood where my task fit in the overall scheme of things, and I also understood why it was being delegated."

Our task as facilitators is to make sure this understanding comes out. Sometimes we have to probe with questions to draw it out. Sometimes we have to show real patience and give young people time to reflect; we don't want to rush them. Sometimes we have time constraints, so we have to ask increasingly direct questions to get them to come up with the answers. Still, we try to avoid asking explicit questions such as, "Was the task clearly defined?"

Usually, you can avoid being that specific by asking questions such as, "What were the key things that made this task work?" and then let them discuss among themselves. You can have them write down the key things that made this task work, specifically related to delegation. Almost always, young people come up with the idea of clearly defining the task and expected result. They often understand why a certain task was given to them personally, which is a powerful realization. Using this approach—getting them to tell you—is far more effective than you telling them, "When you delegate, you need to..."

GRANTING OF AUTHORITY

Along with assignment of duties, delegation involves

granting authority. As mentioned, the delegation we're discussing does not involve menial tasks; instead, it entails *shared authority*. It's about capitalizing on the strengths of each team member to accomplish a common goal by dividing the power. The team captain or project leader recognizes that everyone on the team has value, has something to contribute to the overall team goal. A team has much more power when we engage everyone with this kind of subdivision of decision-making authority.

In the CSDA Youth Sport Leadership model, young people have the opportunity to work together to plan and run a sports league, taking on roles of team managers, coaches, referees, scorers, sport journalists, and so on. Each young person also participates in the tournament as a member of a team. In both cases, there are many opportunities to awaken the leadership skill of delegation. For example, the young person who takes on the role of tournament director works with the organizing committee and in doing so may delegate roles that include developing tournament rules, registering teams, drafting tournament schedules, preparing the venue, and so on. Members of the organizing committee also have the opportunity to work with subcommittees and further apply delegating skills. For example, the committee responsible for registration may work together to agree on the process for team registration and then delegate the task of designing the registration forms to one of the members.

When we delegate tasks to individuals or groups, we are giving them *independence to carry out tasks*, which is another part of granting authority. One of the weaknesses of leaders is intervening after we have delegated a task. This shows a lack of trust in our team members' ability to do what they're supposed to do. Truly giving independence means the leader takes his or her hands off. It means saying to each person on the team, "You are responsible for the closing ceremony," or "You are in charge of coordinating officials for the tournament," or whatever it is.

Another important part of granting authority is *informing the necessary people of the shared authority*. Doing so limits the role confusion and conflict that can potentially arise. For example, if Andre doesn't know that Kim has been given responsibility for liaising with sponsors regarding placement of signage at the venue, he might be confused when Kim talks to him about signage placement and even challenge her authority by saying something like, "Why are you telling me about this? This is not your responsibility."

Letting the entire team know who was given what task also boosts self-esteem. Not only does an individual know that she was delegated a certain task based on her talents, but she also knows the rest of the team understands she was given that leadership role. The rest of the team recognizes the value of each member because everyone knows that each person has been given a specific role to play.

In our work with young people, we demonstrate delegation and the specific subskill of informing the whole team. After we divide the group into their leadership roles—official, journalist, first aider, coach, and so on—we invite colleagues from the sport sector to assist us in facilitating the awakening of knowledge around the specific roles. When the guests arrive, we might tell the group, "This is my team; they're going to help with the youth leadership project. Sam is a sport journalist working with Channel 6, and she is going to work with those who chose the role of sport journalists. Maria is a doctor of sport medicine, and she is going to work with the first aid group. Andre will be working with the coaches, and I'll work with those who selected the role of referees." This demonstrates delegation on a metalevel, or modeling the very skill we're awakening—showing the young people how to delegate and informing others of the tasks each team member has been given.

ESTABLISHING RESPONSIBILITY AND ACCOUNTABILITY

Often when leaders delegate tasks, they stop there; they don't ensure the person has taken responsibility or hold the person accountable. It's a balancing act: although leaders should take their hands off and let their team carry out tasks independently, they also need to establish accountability. In our youth leadership programs, we convey that when someone accepts a delegated task, he or she commits to completing it. The task cannot be passed off to someone else.

The conversation between the leader and the team member might go like this: "James, as we discussed and agreed, I'm delegating this task to you, and this is what we expect at the end of the project. Also, at the end of each day you are responsible for giving me some feedback on how things are going. Then at the end of the week, you will turn in a brief report." Thus, the youth leader builds a sense of responsibility and accountability into the initial delegation conversation, and the individual knows from the beginning that the task is his to complete and that he will be reporting on what he's doing along the way.

Another note on accountability: The greater the person's authority, the greater the level of accountability. The team leader, for example, has the most authority on the team, and he also has the highest level of accountability. Just as the team members check in with the leader, the leader must report to the whole team.

WHAT KIND OF INTERACTION HAPPENS WITH DELEGATION?

MEANINGFUL CONVERSATION

Most importantly, delegation involves meaningful conversation. Leaders do not just assign tasks; they have a conversation with each team member and agree on the assigned role. This approach demonstrates respect for individuals as valued team members, not just passive followers. The meaningful conversation also facilitates negotiation: when a team member feels uncomfortable with a particular task, he or she has an opportunity to discuss it with the leader. The outcome may go one of two ways: the leader may use the opportunity to influence the team member to accept the responsibility, or the team member may persuade the leader to modify or change the task. When young people are involved in the delegation process through meaningful conversation, they are likely to have a greater sense of commitment to complete the task successfully.

TRUST

One of the hardest challenges for leaders with regard to delegation is letting go and trusting a team member to successfully complete the task. Leaders must ensure the job gets done, but they must do so in a way that communicates trust in each team member's ability, responsibility, and so on.

The best way to demonstrate this kind of trust is to periodically check in on team members from a supportive stance. For example, leaders might ask, "How are things coming along with the fund-raiser? Let me know if you need any additional support." It's a delicate balance; leaders must exercise that natural leadership urge to ensure quality control without coming across as mistrusting.

GIVING CLEAR INSTRUCTIONS

Delegation involves explaining what the task entails and what is expected of the person carrying out the task. This explanation should take place through meaningful conversations, not only via email or written instructions. Conversation, where there is opportunity for questions and discussion, ensures clarity.

Delegation is an interactive experience. It's not just about giving instructions; it involves communication to facilitate clarity of expectations, understanding of assigned roles and responsibilities, understanding of individuals' value and place in the overall project, and so on. When leaders delegate, they are responsible for ensuring their teammate fully understands what the task entails. An easy way to determine this is to ask, "Can you tell me what your understanding of the task is? I want to be sure that we're on the same page." It's important for leaders to ask questions like these without sounding condescending.

REFINING THE TASK

One final type of interaction entails feedback from the team members to the leader. As mentioned, leaders are not dictators assigning tasks; they delegate jobs in conversation with others. That discussion continues as the team members fulfill their responsibility. They might come back to the leader with suggestions and questions to refine exactly what the delegated task involves. In doing so, team members add value and ensure the team as a whole fulfills the larger purpose. In conversation with the leader, the team player might say, "I hear what you're saying. I'm thinking it might be better if we did it this way." Team members are not passive implementers of the leader's delegated tasks. They are actively engaged in defining the particulars of the task and how to best carry it out so that it adds to the overall goal or purpose. Leaders strive to create an environment that facilitates this type of interaction—where team members feel comfortable making recommendations.

WAYS TO FACILITATE DELEGATION

As with other leadership skills, the facilitator should not necessarily tell young people how to delegate. The goal is to awaken the skill of delegation through the carefully designed learning experiences—to awaken their understanding of what it means to delegate through the challenges.

There are several ways a facilitator might awaken delegation skills. One approach is to model the delegation behaviors by bringing the youth leaders together and assessing their skill sets, through either a group conversation or a simple skill-set assessment tool on which they tick boxes to identify their level for each skill, from excellent to fair to not so good. At the end, the facilitator can collate the information and then use it to start the delegation conversation: "Ravi, you indicated that you were really good at writing. How do you feel about drafting the letters for sponsors? Sally and George, you both indicated that you were good at art. How do you guys feel about making the posters to promote the event?"

As facilitator, you continue these conversations, clarifying what is expected, demonstrating trust in the youth leaders, and so on. After agreeing on the various roles that each youth leader is assigned, you do the necessary follow-up and provide support as required. At the end of the learning experience you facilitate the reflection dimension by asking the youth leaders general and then specific questions that bring out the key concepts and principles related to delegation. You might say, "Congrats on completing all of these tasks in such a short time. How did we as a team manage to do it? How did you feel when you were asked to take on a particular task? What are some of the things you can do as a leader to strengthen the delegating process?"

Another way to awaken delegation skills involves providing teams with multiple tasks to complete in a relatively short time. Each team may have a list of ten things, and at the end of a specific period (say, fifteen minutes), we then bring the teams in to see how many of the tasks they completed. For the reflection phase (and you may do this as individuals, pairs, small groups, etc.), the young people are asked the same questions presented earlier: "Congrats on completing all of these tasks in such a short time. How did your team manage to do it? How did you feel when you were asked to take on a particular task? What are some of the things that you can do as a leader to strengthen the delegating process?" Note that as with other learning experiences, providing a team with multiple tasks and time limitations can also facilitate other outcomes, including such skills as initiative.

FOR REFLECTION

1. Delegation is a higher-order leadership skill that involves matching the task to the team member with the skill set to effectively carry it out.

2. Consider your own delegation skills. What past experiences have contributed to the development of this leadership skill in you? How have you been using sport to develop delegation skills in young people?

3. What new ideas about delegation did this chapter awaken, and how can you apply these to facilitate youth leadership development in your sport setting?

CHAPTER 10

Decision Making

Decision making is one of the most important leadership skills young people can learn. They will use this skill daily—on the playing field, in the classroom, as part of a work-related team, in relationships, and beyond.

COMPONENTS OF DECISION MAKING

Decision making involves four key components. When making decisions, young people should:

1. Think things through.
2. Make informed decisions.
3. Take responsibility for those decisions.
4. Not limit themselves to what they think can happen.

Leaders don't make hasty decisions. They take their

time and think through the options, seeking additional information as needed to make the best, most informed decision possible. When leaders finally make a decision, they own it; they take responsibility for it no matter what happens afterward.

Many young people struggle with the fourth component; they tend to limit their decisions to what they think can happen. As facilitators, we want to encourage young people to believe that anything is possible—yes, they should balance that belief with pragmatism, as discussed earlier, but they also shouldn't box themselves into thinking, *Because this situation is like this, and this is how it's always done, this must be the best decision.* We want them to think outside the box and make bold decisions. Whatever the situation—organizing a successful local 5K, obtaining a $5,000 sponsorship, or designing an attractive logo—we want young people to be guided by a belief in possibility guarded by reality. We want them to avoid beginning with the thinking that only easy, readily identifiable solutions are possible. If they don't explore what's possible before they make a decision, they don't do justice to their own value. A key part of the decision-making process for young leaders is exploring what is possible.

PROCESS OF DECISION MAKING

The process of decision making involves the *how*: how will

the decision be made, what steps will be taken, who will be involved, and so on. We discuss three options here. No matter which of the three options is used, the leader still strives for the four key components mentioned earlier: thinking through options, making informed decisions, taking responsibility, and exploring new possibilities rather than being limited.

DELEGATION

One option is to *delegate* the decision making—a powerful approach to facilitate among young people. Delegating the decision making involves trust and recognizing the value in team members. A youth leader might say to her team, "OK, you guys are the subcommittee and you're responsible for deciding on the format for the tournament," or "Jamie, you decide on a sponsorship strategy," or whatever it is. The team leader does not make the decision; she delegates the decision-making responsibility to an individual or group. In doing so, the team leader empowers her teammates: she gives them a leadership role in the overall project. They aren't just following directions; they're making decisions that will affect the outcome of the project.

> **REMINDER**
>
> Before the youth leader can delegate decision-making tasks on her own, she needs to understand the principles involved in good decision making. As mentioned earlier and illustrated in figure 10.1, this understanding is initiated in the first phase of the CSDA model. As the young people move into the Practice phase, they have opportunities to execute the skill independently in a semi-controlled environment. Finally, they move into the Application phase, where they apply the decision-making skill in an open environment without controls of the coach or facilitator.

When the team leader delegates decision making to team members, he follows the same guidelines for delegation discussed in chapter 9. The leader assigns decision-making tasks as part of a conversation with the various team members, and those team members accept responsibility for getting the tasks done. This process results in a powerful learning experience for all involved. The leader learns to have faith in his team, and the team members feel the power of having a decision-making leadership role.

DISCUSSION

The second option is to *discuss*—not only with the team members but also with outside sources of information. The leader is responsible for making the final decision, but beforehand, he discusses options with others and gathers information to help in deciding what to do. Leaders should

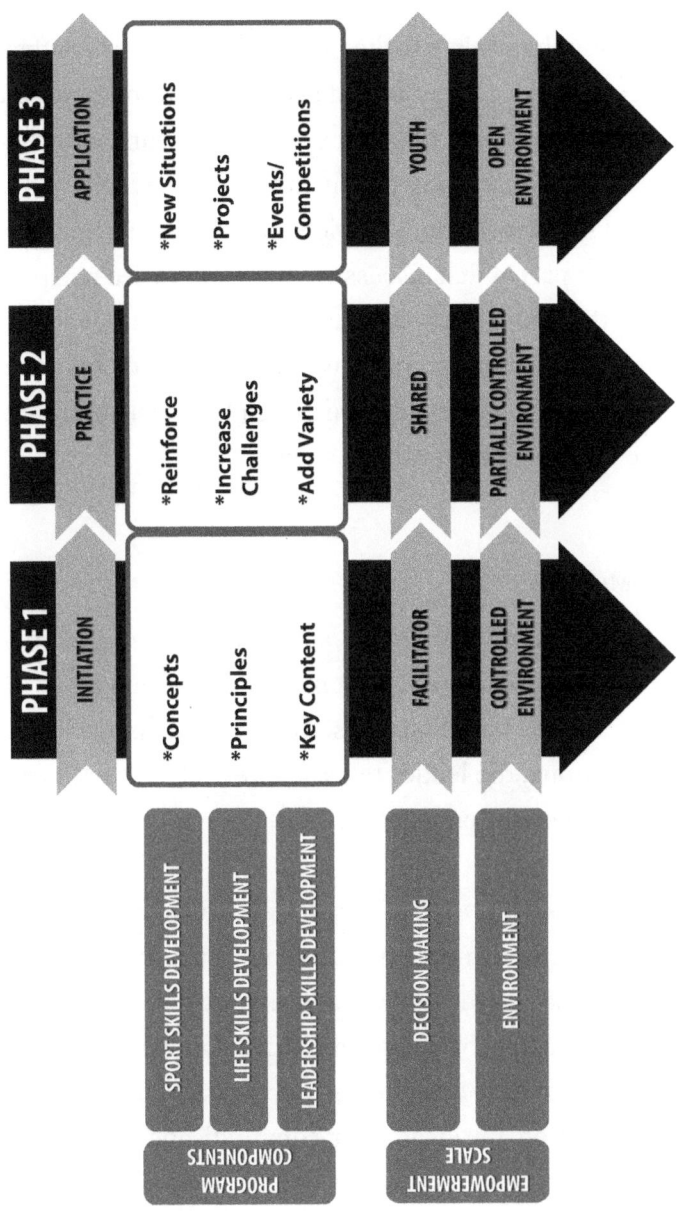

Figure 10.1: CSDA Youth Sport Leadership Model with Empowerment Scale

not limit themselves to the information they have or that their team has. They should also seek external sources. Discussion should take place within the team and with people, organizations, and institutions outside the team. Through conversation, new ideas arise; the more people who are part of that discussion, the more varied perspectives the leader has to consider in making a final decision. The leader cannot come up with every angle on his own; discussions like these ensure the leader is well informed and has considered various angles.

DEMOCRACY

The third approach I call *democracy*, or coming to consensus. The leader does not make the decision alone in this case; it's based on votes. After a team discussion of the options, the leader takes a vote and goes with the consensus—the popular decision.

Before taking a vote, the leader must ensure the team has engaged in ample discussion of the pros and cons of the ideas on the table, that everyone has a chance to voice concerns, bring up alternative options, and so on. We want to have an educated popular vote. During this conversation, the ideas about communication discussed in chapter 5 come into play—specifically, engaging in respectful communication and reaching a shared pool of understanding so that the best decision can be made.

Once a decision is reached, we talk about everyone taking ownership of it. This decision is made as a team, and because each person involved in the decision is part of the team, each person supports that final decision, even if he or she was outvoted. Taking ownership in this way involves another leadership skill already discussed: adaptability.

STEPS IN A DECISION-MAKING LEARNING EXPERIENCE

As mentioned, participants engaged in the CSDA Youth Sport Leadership program move through three phases in the process of awakening leadership skills—from Initiation to Practice to Application. And as they move through these phases, there is a gradual transition of decision-making power, shifting from a coach- or facilitator-controlled environment to an open environment where the youth leaders, now equipped with their leadership skills, are empowered to make decisions without the influence of the coach or facilitator.

The Empowerment Scale section of the model illustrates the shift in decision-making power through the course of the program. In this chapter, we discuss decision making as a leadership skill; figure 10.2 shows how decision making is also a key part of the empowerment process involved in youth leadership development in the CSDA model. Leadership involves having the power to make decisions; this section of the CSDA model emphasizes the shift in decision-making power, from adults to young people.

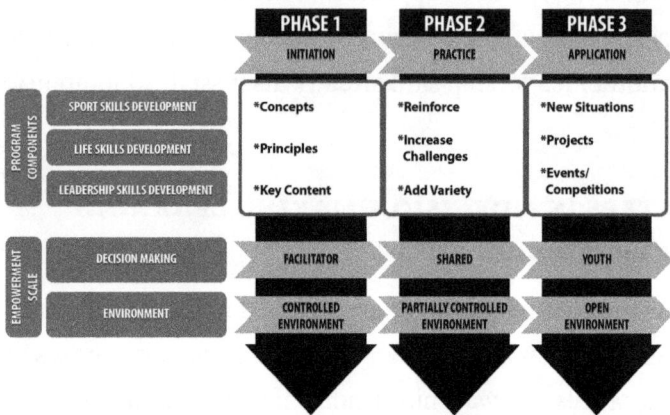

Figure 10.2: Decision Making as Part of the Empowerment Process

In phase 1 (see figure 10.3), coaches and facilitators make decisions in a way that shows young people how and why decisions are being made. As facilitators, we're not just making decisions because we're in charge; we're modeling the leadership skill we want the young people to learn and practice. For example, you might come in the second day of a weeklong program and say something like, "Yesterday, we did serving to targets, and we could do that again today. However, some of you were hitting the targets, but you had bad technique, so instead, we're going to focus on technique today." Thus, you're telling the young people what you're doing and why. You're modeling informed decision making and you're also showing respect to the young people by explaining why—you're not just giving them an order and expecting them to follow it. As we model the skill, young people learn the basis for making informed decisions.

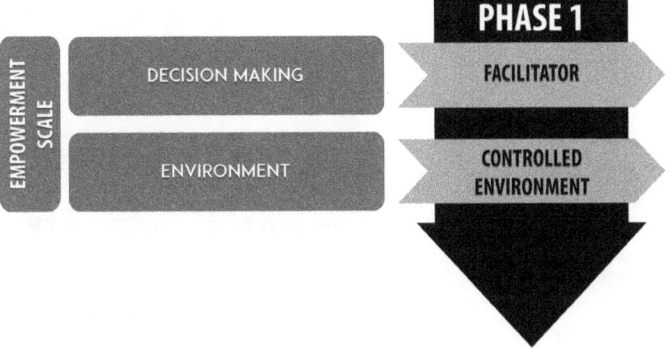

Figure 10.3: First Phase of Empowerment Scale

In phase 2, coaches and facilitators start shifting the decision-making power to the young people. In this partially controlled environment (see figure 10.4), decision making is shared. Rather than making the decision and explaining our reasoning as in phase 1, we might give the young people a set number of options and let them decide. For example, we might say, "Do you want to hit to targets, or do you want to play a mini volleyball game?" or "Are we going to work in teams, or are we going work individually?" We throw out these options, and then we have a conversation—either as a whole group or in teams. You might tell them to discuss in their groups the pros and cons of each potential experience—of working in pairs versus working in fives, or dividing up into leadership roles (official, coach, journalist, etc.) and working in those groups versus working in their teams. When they come back, ask them what they decided and why. This gets the young people thinking about making meaningful, informed decisions; reflecting on the process as a whole; and so on.

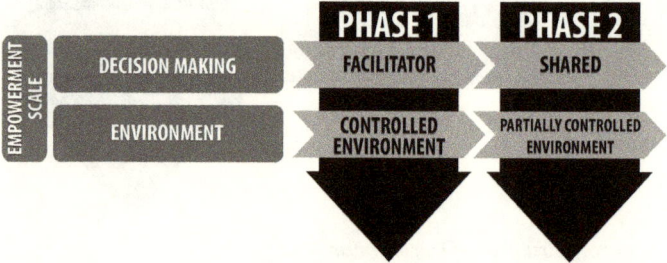

Figure 10.4: Second Phase of Empowerment Scale

Because this phase involves shared decision making, when the groups tell us what they decided, we may say, "I hear what you're saying about this activity. I think that's good. Let's take a vote to come to a final decision." Thus, we as facilitators still control the decision making to some extent.

In phase 3 (see figure 10.5), the control shifts entirely to the young people. We might say to the group, "Let us know what you will be working on today"—and this applies to sport skills, life skills, and other leadership skills. We don't give choices or options at this point; young people make all decisions. We might say, "Let me know what format you will be using for the tournament," rather than, "Do you want to do a round robin or knockoff?" This shift of control and decision-making power can only happen if we have created learning experiences during the preceding sessions that give them opportunities to make decisions and think about the decision-making process. As facilitators, we might ask the young people, "What did you decide? Why did you come to that decision? What are the pros and cons? How did you come to a final decision? Did everyone have input? How did you feel about that decision?" These conversations are part of the reflection after the challenge.

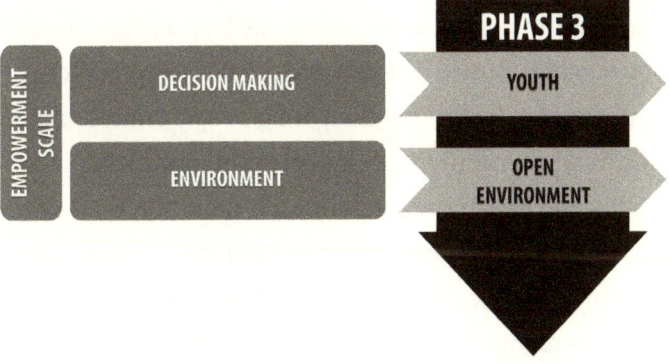

Figure 10.5: Third Phase of Empowerment Scale

As facilitators, we should not judge young people's decisions. It's not a matter of right or wrong but, more importantly, that they learn from the process through thoughtful reflection.

HOW DO TEAMS MAKE DECISIONS?

There are many ways to make decisions as a team. Different contexts call for different methods. For instance, sometimes we want the vote to be anonymous, so we use a blind vote method: have everyone write down their choice, put it in a hat, and then tally up the votes together. If the context allows, you can also have people raise their hands in support of one option or the other.

We use these decision-making methods in many situations—everything from choosing the tournament format to picking a fund-raising idea to figuring out the best defensive strategy to use against a particular team. Anything that requires a decision in the course of a program or practice we can throw out to the team—that's the learning experience you engage them in. We can add or take away challenges with the goal being that the young people learn to make informed decisions through conversation with their teammates. We give them guidelines, but we don't tell them how to come to a decision. After they make a decision, we encourage reflection by asking questions such as, "What did your team use to make a decision? Did everyone contribute ideas? Is there another way you could have come to a decision?" These questions bring them to the information already presented in this book about making informed decisions—they discover it themselves; we don't tell them.

Remember, young people don't learn skills in a vacuum. In

the process of awakening leadership skills such as decision making, we also bring out life skills such as respect. We might point out that coming to a decision isn't a competition; the goal isn't to make the right decision and then brag about it/rub it in the face of the other team. Likewise, if participants don't agree with the decision made, they can disagree respectfully, not with name-calling or rude language or comments such as, "What kind of goal is that? Just a waste of time."

Communication skills also come into play when young people explain why they disagree or how they might be upset that the group didn't go with their idea. As facilitators, we can help them learn to make their point respectfully. One conversation might be, "If your team didn't go with your idea, how did that make you feel? Why? How could we have done this better as a group?" As we have a reflective discussion, key points come out about being respectful to everyone involved in the decision-making process.

One decision-making opportunity in our youth sport leadership programs involves choosing a team name and logo. We often have individuals pick a name and logo, and then discuss it in pairs, and then as a group of four. The process necessarily involves negotiation, communication, and finally, coming to a decision. In the decision-making process, the team considers, "Does this name really reflect who we are and what we want to say about our team? Does the logo represent that name in a clear way?" Answering these questions helps each team come to an informed decision that each member can own and support.

There are many other opportunities to develop decision making as a team. In the context of a tournament, young people could decide the tournament format, how many teams, how many people on a team, the scoring system, rules, and so on. On individual teams, the players could decide on a defensive strategy or training schedule, whether they will play a practice game, whether they will do mental preparation as a team, and so on. All of those things and more require choices that can be facilitated through learning experiences designed by coaches and teachers. The key is to introduce decision-making experiences, awaken the skills needed to make informed decisions independently and in groups, and then gradually pass the decision-making power on to the young people.

HOW DO YOUTH LEADERS PUT DECISION MAKING INTO PRACTICE?

To put decision making into practice, youth leaders need to take initiative—a leadership skill discussed in the next chapter. Young people must understand that if they are leading a team or organization, they can't sit on the fence and wait for someone else to act; they are responsible for making decisions and then acting on those decisions.

At this point, many groups fall apart: A decision needs to be made and no one will make it, so people wait around wondering, *How are we going to do this? What's the plan?* In these situations, the group is not moving forward; they're going around in circles and sometimes even sliding backward and getting stuck because no one will make a decision.

A key truth to communicate to young leaders is the need to commit to making a decision. They can't sit around and wait for someone else to make the decision for them. Young leaders need to step up and say, "This is what we're going to do." That decision may involve delegating tasks to team members or having a team discussion to reach consensus, but the bottom line is, the leader has to put the decision-making process in motion.

The leader doesn't have to consult her team for every little issue; sometimes the leader just decides. In such cases, the leader should still engage her team in conversation so each person understands why she made the decision. For example, if the team leader decides to cancel practice, she comes to the team to explain why. Or if the leader delegates logo design to Stephen and Tim, she tells the team that this is what she did.

WHAT KEY LIFE SKILLS DO YOUNG PEOPLE LEARN IN THE CONTEXT OF DECISION MAKING?

As they learn to make decisions, young people gain other leadership qualities as well. Leaders learn to take responsibility for the consequences of their decisions, whatever they are. Even if a decision is made in conversation with others, is well informed, and is based on thorough research, things may still go wrong. A leader owns the decision and the result and learns from his mistakes.

In addition, a leader makes the necessary adjustments so he doesn't make the same mistake twice. He doesn't focus on blaming someone or something for why it didn't work as planned. The leader knows, "This is what we did. This is why we did it. Unfortunately, we didn't take ___ into consideration, and something went awry. Next time, we'll do this." If possible, he stops the process and makes a correction immediately. This action brings in another leadership skill: adaptability. The leader looks for ways to fix the situation now that will improve the current process.

In some cases, leaders may delegate a responsibility and in hindsight realize that wasn't the best match of task and skill set. The leader now has an opportunity to address the situation with the individuals—not harshly but with respect. He can treat it as a learning experience—for himself and his team members—and talk to team members about what could have been done differently.

Young leaders learn respect, adaptability, communication, and more.

WAYS TO FACILITATE DECISION MAKING

As with each of the leadership skills, we facilitate decision making in a phased process based on carefully designed learning experiences. We don't tell young people what decisions to make or how to make them; instead, we create opportunities for them to make informed decisions using one of the approaches mentioned earlier: delegation, discussion, or democracy. As young people engage in decision-making challenges, we debrief and get them to think about and verbalize what decisions they made and why they made them.

As mentioned, decision-making opportunities are readily available. We can have young people make decisions about everything from a team name to practice times to a defensive strategy to materials to use in building a goal. Oftentimes, these learning experiences provide more challenges than we as facilitators plan for, which gives young people real, authentic opportunities to practice leadership skills.

One learning experience we use involves choosing a 5K route. In Trinidad, we often do school 5Ks, and we will run through residential areas because they are quieter and have less traffic. Young people pick a route, and sometimes they put a note in people's mailboxes or we drive through the area with a megaphone to let people know about the upcoming event in their neighborhood. However, we always run the risk of having a conflicting event the same day because we can't know everything that's going on in each neighborhood.

On one occasion, the young people made a decision and planned out a safe 5K route. On the day of the race, they discovered that someone in the neighborhood was having a wedding. How could they have planned for that? They couldn't, and that's one of the realities of decision making: No matter how much preparation you do, no matter how well informed the decision is, something can always go wrong. Timing devices can malfunction, volunteers might not show up, other events might conflict. When unplanned things happen during a learning experience, we have the chance to facilitate real-life, hands-on learning. We can help the young people own their decision, make the best of the situation in front of them, and later reflect on it. Considering questions such as "What could we do differently next time ahead of the race?" and "Could we have handled it differently once we realized there was a problem?" will help young people learn from the current situation and make better informed decisions in the future.

FOR REFLECTION

1. Decision making is the ultimate sign of being a leader; if you're not making decisions, you're not embracing leadership. Young people need to learn the skill of informed decision making, as it will affect every area of their lives.

2. Consider your own decision-making skills. What past experiences have contributed to the development of this leadership skill in you? How have you been using sport to develop decision-making skills in young people?

3. What new ideas about decision making did this chapter awaken, and how can you apply these to facilitate youth leadership development in your sport setting?

CHAPTER 11

Initiative

The difference between leaders and followers can be seen in terms of initiative. Followers may look at a challenge and discuss options for solving it, but ultimately, they don't take any action; they wait for someone to tell them what to do. Leaders, on the other hand, act. They figure out what needs to be done and they do it without waiting for direction. Initiative is a key leadership skill.

In one of our youth leadership programs a few years back, we were meeting inside for the day. Groups were taking turns doing presentations, but the projector wasn't working properly. While most of the young people tried to fix the broken projector, one participant got up and left the room. He came back a couple of minutes later and summoned everyone into the next room, where the projector was working, and we continued with the presentations.

That's the perfect picture of initiative. No one said, "Hey, Matthew, could you go check the projector in another room?" And he didn't wait to be asked. Matthew thought of a solution and he acted on it.

THE FOUNDATION OF INITIATIVE

Initiative is really a combination of several other leadership skills, especially adaptability, resourcefulness, and getting things done. In order to show initiative, you have to be open to other possibilities and solutions; you need to be willing to think outside the box, or beyond the boundary as we say in cricket. And then you make a decision and act.

There is no initiative if there is no action. In our programs, we often use a picture that shows three tadpoles sitting on a lily pad in a pond. We show the illustration and ask the question, "Three tadpoles sitting on a lily pad. One decides to jump off. How many remain?" The question provokes lots of discussion but eventually leads to the point that making a decision to jump off is not the same as jumping. We often decide to do things but never get them done. Initiative is about taking action.

HOW LEADERS DEMONSTRATE INITIATIVE

Leaders have a responsibility to model initiative as well as to encourage initiative among team members. The following are some key ways in which leaders may demonstrate these behaviors:

1. Team leaders continuously seek out information about challenges that individuals or the team as a whole may be experiencing and demonstrate initiative by identifying possible solutions and acting on them. By exhibiting initiative, leaders provide a model for team members to follow.
2. Team leaders create an environment where team members feel safe to take risks. Sometimes initiative involves taking risks that may lead to success—or not. If the environment is not conducive to risk-taking, there is likely to be less initiative among team members. Of course, this risk-taking behavior needs to be balanced with common sense to avoid losing sight of the purpose in the effort to think outside the box.
3. Team leaders encourage team members to support others who are already demonstrating initiative. This enhances the value of initiative and validates the efforts of those taking initiative. For example, the leader might say, "Great job by Jaime in organizing the used sports equipment drive. It would be great if others could join him to extend the project for another month."

WAYS TO FACILITATE INITIATIVE

As with the other leadership skills, we facilitate initiative by designing experiences, creating challenges that provide opportunities for young people to engage in the skill itself, and helping young people reflect on what they've learned. Any challenge we give young people will have built-in opportunities to show initiative. If they are working as a group on a task, some people will be working and some will be sitting around and observing. This is the perfect chance to have a conversation—to reflect on what's happening in the midst of the challenge, to bring out how initiative is or is not being demonstrated. Let's say the challenge is to build a bridge given limited supplies. We can talk to the group about the two ways people are approaching the bridge building: some are waiting around for instructions, and some recognized that in order to build the bridge, they need posts, so they started making posts. Then we bring out that those who started building showed initiative.

Another way to facilitate initiative is to throw out a need and see who responds. For example, if we happen to be in the gym for practice, I might say, "Wow, this gym really needs a cleanup," and then go on with what we're doing. We don't assign the task; we don't say what needs cleaning or how it should be cleaned or where the cleaning supplies are kept. We just provide the opportunity for initiative. When we come back the next day, I might say, "I noticed that two of your teammates came in the afternoon and started cleaning the gym and put the equipment away," and lead into a conversation about how their actions showed initiative.

Other challenges can be thrown out in the same way. The key is to make it something real—that is, something that really needs to get done in the context of the practice or learning experience or whatever. Here are a few examples:

- If you're playing football, you could mention that the field isn't lined because the guy who usually does it is sick.
- If you're playing basketball, you could say something like, "Look at your hands. See how dirty they get after playing a game? Must be the basketballs."
- If you're playing volleyball, you could mention that you can't start practice until the nets are up.

If we repeatedly throw out challenges like these, we help young people develop a habit of responding with initiative; there will be less and less guidance on our part and more and more initiative on theirs. At some point, we don't even need to mention that the gym looks dirty; the young people notice on their own and take care of it.

Many of the experiences we use to facilitate initiative also bring out the personal and social responsibility values promoted by Hellison. Through these challenges, young people see it as their responsibility to keep the gym clean, put the equipment away, line the fields, and so on. Responsibility is a life skill or value that is closely linked to initiative and other leadership skills.

You will probably find that some children see right through your observation about the dirty gym or unlined field. They know you're deliberately putting these challenges out there. That's OK; some young people are just more intuitive.

As we've mentioned, facilitation is part art, part science, knowing when and how to present situations to awaken the intended skill. If the field really hasn't been marked, I could make this observation and ask for volunteers, but this would work on responsibility more than initiative. You might start here early in the program and then work up to the point where you throw out an observation and finally to the point where a young person comes to you and says, "Coach, I noticed Chris isn't here and he usually lines the field, but we have a game tomorrow. I'm organizing people to get the field marked." That's the highest level; that's where we want young people to be by the end of our programs. But we can only get there if we start with experiences that awaken the idea that they could have noticed the unlined field and done something about it. It's empowering for young people to make this realization, to know that they can bring value to this situation and that they don't have to wait for someone to tell them what to do. They're smart and they can make those decisions on their own. That's leadership. That's what we're trying to communicate.

We can manipulate these experiences to work on other skills as well. For example, you might have a few young people who pick up on the initiative skill right away. You could pull one of them aside and say, "Jacob, I know you're always using initiative and helping out, but I need you to help me develop that behavior among your friends. What can you do?" You're now giving Jacob an opportunity to use leadership skills such as communication and delegation, and you're also giving other young people a different opportunity in which to learn initiative. As mentioned, we must monitor the learning experiences. If some participants are not catching on, we need to modify the challenge so that they do—in this case, by involving another young person in the awakening process.

Another way to manipulate the environment to force initiative is to deliberately not show up at the beginning of a session and see how the young people respond. For example, you may have told the group earlier in the day, "We have a game at 4:00 p.m. and we need to start right away." And then you don't show up at 4:00 p.m., and there's no net on the court. You left the net out, but someone has to put it up. You can watch from a distance to see what happens.

You have created a scenario, a learning experience, but for it to be meaningful, you also have to facilitate a conversation afterward. In this situation, someone may or may not put up the net before you show up; either way, you have a discussion afterward. If the net is up, you could discuss it from a positive perspective and say something like, "Guys, I want to thank Philip and Grace for putting the net up yesterday. Do you want to tell us why you did that?" Then you bring the conversation to the topic of leadership: "What do their actions tell us about Philip and Grace?"

On the other hand, if no one put up the net, you would have a different conversation: "Guys, we had a game yesterday, but it didn't happen. Why not? What could you have done to change the situation and make the game happen?" You don't have control over the young people's responses and you can't predict what they will do, but you can use their responses to communicate the skill or value. Even if they didn't do what you hoped and you feel disappointment, don't treat the conversation as punishment. It's a learning experience.

FOR REFLECTION

1. Initiative involves a combination of other leadership skills—adaptability, resourcefulness, and decision making in particular. It's important for young people to realize that even if they are not the appointed leader, they have the power to add value and resolve challenges by using initiative.

2. Consider your own initiative skills. What past experiences have contributed to the development of this leadership skill in you? How have you been using sport to develop initiative in young people?

3. What new ideas about initiative did this chapter awaken, and how can you apply these to facilitate youth leadership development in your sport setting?

CHAPTER 12

Getting Things Done

Leaders get things done. They use initiative, adapt when required, delegate, make decisions—in short, they use all the leaderships skills we've discussed to successfully complete the task. As mentioned earlier, we want young people to use their leadership power for good. When they apply the skills presented in this book, they have the power to mobilize other young people in their communities to help feed the homeless or to collect and distribute relief supplies to families who may have been affected by floods or other natural disasters, to plan and organize community sporting events, or to lobby for better sporting facilities in their community. Young people have the power to make a difference.

As mentioned earlier, getting things done doesn't necessarily mean actually doing them. If someone is responsible for making sure the team has drinks after practice, that individual doesn't have to physically bring out the ice chest; he or she can assign the task to someone else on the team. In this sense, getting things done is a *personal responsibility*: the team captain or project leader or player assigned to the task has to make sure it's accomplished.

Getting things done is also a collective *team responsibility*. In the previous chapter, we gave the example of a volleyball game not happening because the net wasn't put up. In that situation, the team knew they had a game at 4:00 p.m. They were responsible for making that happen, which in this case meant putting up the net so they could play.

Finally, getting things done is a *social responsibility*. We want young people to learn that we all have a responsibility to each other, to the community, and to society in general. In life, we have obligations to fulfill but not at the expense of being personally or socially irresponsible. We don't want youth to use any means necessary to get things done. Whether at school, at home, at work, or on a team, fulfilling a role or completing a task should happen in the context of social responsibility—that is, taking care of the environment, watching out for others, abiding by the rules, and so on.

GETTING THINGS DONE: THE INFLUENCE OF DAVID ALLEN'S BOOK

In many organizations, people sit in meetings and plan things but then feel like nothing is accomplished. So they go back to another meeting and talk some more and do all sorts of things, but still the actual project sits uncompleted.

This reality came out in our own conversations at CSDA. We felt like we were doing a lot of things but not really getting things done. Then one of our staff members introduced us to a book called *Getting Things Done* by David Allen. We bought copies for the entire staff, and we started having our own workshops based on this book.

The book helped us put tasks in categories using a matrix with four quadrants:

1. Important and urgent
2. Important, not urgent
3. Not important, not urgent
4. Not important but urgent

This matrix helped us organize and prioritize projects, tasks, and so on. This helped us determine what we were actually going to do each day.

Allen's book also gave us a step-by-step process for getting things done that we still follow today. This process forms the basis of our youth programs when we present the notion that leaders apply all of the skills outlined in the previous chapters to actually do something—or rather, to get something (meaningful) done!

THE PROCESS
1. Identify the Purpose

In other words, why are we doing this? What is the main outcome we want for this particular project? We keep that purpose in the back of our minds, and as we engage in different tasks, we ask ourselves, "Is this relevant to the purpose?" When we ascertain the purpose of any task or project, we are better able to determine if we fulfilled that purpose at the end of the process. When we are unclear about purpose, we may be busy doing but not necessarily achieving anything meaningful.

2. Brainstorm

After we identify the project's purpose, we brainstorm. Everyone throws out their ideas for how to accomplish the purpose. At this point, we capture *all* of the ideas on a whiteboard. We don't evaluate or ask questions or try to figure out how an idea would work; we just write them down. This helps us to keep all of our options open, and the brainstorming as a group often facilitates new ideas as we build on the imagination of others.

3. Clarify

After brainstorming, we clarify ideas as needed. This is where team members can ask questions to understand someone's idea. For example, someone might ask, "What do you mean when you say you want to have a skills festival?" This element of the process facilitates thoughtful analysis of which ideas can best meet the intended outcomes. Part of the clarification process also explores the cost, feasibility, effectiveness, and efficiency of the options and matches that with available resources. At the end of the day, we must clearly see the process of implementing each idea and how it could lead to success—to fulfillment of the intended purpose.

4. Organize and Prioritize

After brainstorming and clarifying, we organize and prioritize, focusing on which ideas fit with the purpose we have already identified. We don't toss ideas that don't work for the current project; we file them away for future reference. Usually, there are several ideas that may be incorporated to achieve a specific outcome, and sometimes there are subtasks within the overall project. Organizing and prioritizing the ideas and subtasks helps us to focus using the important/urgent matrix presented earlier.

5. Decide

At the end of this brainstorming-clarifying-prioritizing process, we decide on the ideas we are going to implement. It's a group decision; everyone on the team is involved in making it, and thus, everyone takes ownership of the decision once it's made.

6. Agree on the Next Action

Before the meeting breaks up, we always agree on the next action. Identifying what to do next is the most important part of our collective engagement. Once we agree on the next actions, we attach a time line and identify the individual or individuals responsible. Then at the next meeting, each person reports on his or her task, and again, we decide on the next actions until the project is finally complete.

THE RESULT

This process is effective because the whole team is engaged from beginning to end. As a result, all team members take ownership of the decision, and thus, they all make a commitment to see the next actions completed. This is a key element of getting things done: having staff or students or team members feel ownership for each project because they have been involved in the entire decision-making process. They are committed to getting it done.

As we move through the process, from identifying purpose to clarifying it to making a decision and acting on it, we also engage in reflection. That reflective process is an ongoing activity.

APPLICATION WITH YOUNG PEOPLE

When we present this skill to young people, we use the same format that we use for other leadership skills: we design an experience, engage participants in a challenge, modify the challenge as needed, and debrief on learning. During the challenge, young people go through the preceding steps—identify the purpose, brainstorm, and so on—in an effort to get things done.

For example, the challenge might be to organize a sporting event. To get things done as a team, the young people first have to determine the purpose of the event: is it to make sure everyone gets to participate, or is it to see who is the best at that particular school? Those are two different purposes, which will result in two different types of sporting events. Then we guide the young people through the process of moving from idea to action. As a group, they brainstorm, clarify, organize, decide, and act; because everyone is engaged in the whole process, everyone is committed to making it happen.

As mentioned, young people in our programs learn skills

in three phases: Initiation, Practice, Application. Through each phase, they take on authentic sport leadership roles—journalist, coach, manager, first aider, and so on—and learn skills in the context of those roles. The tournament at the end of the program is the Application phase where they actually perform the roles without guidance from the adults.

Prior to the actual tournament, participants meet in subcommittees according to their roles—all the journalists meet together, all the coaches, and so on. Each subcommittee has certain tasks to complete in the context of the tournament, and they use the getting-things-done process to accomplish those tasks. This tournament setting provides many authentic situations to apply this leadership skill because the young people are running a real tournament—they are setting up a *real* schedule, for *real* teams to play in *real* games with *real* officials—and therefore they really have to get things done. The process outlined earlier effectively helps young people move from ideas to actions in this authentic context.

GETTING THINGS DONE CONSISTENTLY

To get things done consistently, we must develop positive habits. When our staff at CSDA started working through the book *Getting Things Done*, we began two new processes: a manila folder system to organize our ideas and multiple whiteboards for group brainstorming sessions. Only one of these processes developed into a habit—the whiteboards. People loved the group engagement and conversation that went with brainstorming on the boards, so that action has continued.

Developing habits is not easy; it takes time and effort. In order to make a change in behavior and thought processes, we have to really want the end result: the new skill or clean bedroom or the organized closet or whatever it is. If we don't really want it or don't see the value in it, we won't put in the effort.

As facilitators, we can help young people form lasting habits in a couple of ways. We can start by incorporating habit-developing opportunities in the learning experiences. When we do so, we link the idea of developing habits to the leadership skill of getting things done. We can start with awareness; that is, we can help young people be aware of things they want to get done on a personal level—earn better grades, keep their room clean, exercise more often—and find out where they are with those habits. For example, the conversation might go like this:

> Facilitator: "Where are you with this new reading habit? You said you wanted to start reading more books, so how are you doing?"

Young person: "I'm reading on my own only once every three weeks."

Facilitator: "That's not how often you wanted to read, is it? You wanted to do this every day. Now that you're aware of where you are, what decision can you make in terms of developing the habit you want?"

This last question leads the young person to make a commitment, which is a key part of developing a lasting habit and thus getting things done. After we become aware that we're not doing what we said we wanted to do, we can make a decision to do something different. Developing a habit involves saying to yourself, "OK, this is something I really want to do. I want to learn to play guitar, so I'm making a decision to practice."

After young people make a commitment to do something, we can help them identify triggers—the ideas, actions, or events that prompt them to do the thing they've committed to do. To figure out triggers, young people might ask themselves, "What gets me to practice my guitar?" or "What will push me to read more often?" For example, my wife loves to run, but sometimes after work, she's tired and feels unmotivated. As soon as she hears her running music, however, she catches the vibe, puts on her running shoes, and gets on the treadmill. Music triggers her running habit.

Once young people identify their triggers, they need to pull them—take action. And they need to keep pulling those triggers until the response becomes automatic. This is how a habit is formed: when we are triggered, we take action and we keep doing so until the action is automatic and we don't even think about it.

Sometimes young people need rewards to keep them motivated, especially in the early stages of developing a habit. Ideally, these rewards should be intrinsic—something inherent in the activity itself. For example, after exercising, some people feel happy and content—a kind of "runner's high." That's an intrinsic reward. Other people don't feel euphoric after exercise, so they might need external rewards to keep them committed to their new habit—for example, two squares of dark chocolate or a ten-minute foot rub if they run three miles twice a week.

We can also encourage young people to tell others about the habit they're trying to form. By doing so, they create their own little support team. Members of the group can encourage one another. They know one another's triggers and help one another respond to them and take action.

WHAT DOES BALANCE HAVE TO DO WITH GETTING THINGS DONE?

If a team is clicking, if they're working well together and

getting things done, it's easy to become really immersed in the work—too immersed sometimes. When this happens, our work-life balance may sometimes get thrown off.

We've had this happen at our CSDA office; people become so excited about a project and they get more and more done, but they also end up spending excessive amounts of time working. We do want to get things done, but we also want people to have a meaningful life experience. At the CSDA office, we encouraged people to get up from their desks and walk around or go hit a few golf balls into the net outside (yeah, we have one of those). We also had a basketball hoop outside, and sometimes we'd play after work or during breaks. One staff member enjoyed organizing team fitness challenges using pedometers to determine who had the most steps in a month, as well as personal fitness challenges that have nothing to do with work. People don't have to be at their desks all day. They're responsible for getting things done, but we also want them to be healthy and happy.

This is an important lesson to share with young people: Life involves more than going to school, getting a degree, getting a job, and then work, work, work. A truly meaningful life needs balance. We don't have to spend a lot of time at work to get things done; we can learn to work more efficiently so we have time to enjoy hobbies, sports, volunteering, and other interests.

GUIDELINES FOR GETTING THINGS DONE

As facilitators, we can awaken this skill in the same way we have awakened other leadership skills: design learning experiences, engage young people in the experience, modify the challenge as needed, and help youth reflect on what they've learned. The key knowledge we want to communicate in this case is an understanding of how to brainstorm, clarify, decide, and move from idea to action in order to get things done.

As you facilitate this specific leadership skill, keep three words in mind: simplicity, structure, and support.

SIMPLICITY

When working with young people, it's important to keep our instructions simple. Likewise, we also want young people to keep their solutions simple when they work on challenges. Thinking of simple solutions rather than complicated ones is an important subskill in getting things done.

Many complex problems can be solved with simple interventions. Note that simplicity does not mean that they are unimaginative and unoriginal. Often, simple solutions are creative and innovative. Most importantly, your solution should fulfill its intended purpose, and it should do so as simply and as efficiently as possible.

Story about the Magic Rope

Childhood obesity is a noncommunicable disease, just like cancer or diabetes. For years, doctors, politicians, philanthropists, and government officials have been trying to come up with the best solutions to prevent childhood obesity and other noncommunicable diseases. At CSDA, we've come up with a simple solution to reduce childhood obesity: the magic rope! The magic rope is a jump rope, and it helps facilitate regular participation in a moderately vigorous physical activity that can be done daily in both indoor and outdoor spaces. We use the jump rope because it's a little more inclusive than, say, a football. Both boys and girls jump rope. You don't have to be an expert football or basketball player or have a certain skill set; anyone can jump rope. We also point out that a jump rope costs very little.

If we can just get kids moving, we will make great strides toward solving the childhood obesity issue. Research shows that if we develop habits of participation in physical activity starting at age five, six, and seven, kids are more likely to be active for the rest of their lives. The jump rope is one way to do this, and it's such a simple solution that it's often overlooked.

In our leadership programs, we communicate that young people should not ignore the simple answers; sometimes they are more effective than the complicated ones and require less time and money.

KISS Principle

You may have heard of the KISS principle: Keep it simple, stupid. By *simple* we don't mean less meaningful or effective. Simple just means less complicated. The reality is that the less complicated a task or solution is, the more likely it is to find success.

Using the jump rope, for example, it is easy for us to measure body mass index (BMI) before and after implementing jump rope activities. Likewise, if we use pedometers to count steps, we have a simple way of comparing activity levels from day to day, week to week, and so on.

STRUCTURE

When facilitating experiences around getting things done, it's also important to pay attention to structure. The structure itself should be simple, not a complex series of steps, layers, and dimensions. Whatever we're working on, we try to limit the structure to three to five steps or actions. That's not a rule, but we try to avoid processes that involve more than five steps or actions (three being our preference). A simple example of a structure for a project might look like this:

- Phase 1: planning and meeting with key stakeholders
- Phase 2: awareness campaign
- Phase 3: training volunteers

- Phase 4: implementation
- Phase 5: reporting

Structure also helps with your day-to-day functioning. Here are three simple guidelines for developing a structure to facilitate getting things done:

1. Identify times for specific tasks—for example, exercise time, reading time, work time, and so on.
2. Identify spaces for specific tasks—for example, coffee shop for meetings, desk for answering emails, and so on.
3. Determine how much time you want to spend on specific tasks—for example, sixty minutes for exercise, forty-five minutes for emails, one hour for new reading material, and so on.

Having structure facilitates better organization and can lead to getting more done. Note that you can adjust these guidelines as you enhance the structures for getting things done.

SUPPORT

I didn't come up with the following statement, but it accurately describes this idea of support: "If you want to walk fast, walk alone; if you want to walk far, walk with someone." When we work on challenges and come up with solutions with the support of others, the experience is fuller and richer, and it ultimately leads to more success.

In our organization, I have acted on my own many times because I just wanted to get something done and accomplished to my standard. In some ways, that route is less complicated, because I don't have to wait for others, but it's also limited. When the team works on a task, the experience is richer and the outcome better; there is an added value inherent in working with the support of others.

> **FOR REFLECTION**
>
> 1. Leaders use their leadership skills (communication, teamwork, resourcefulness, adaptability, delegation, decision making, and initiative) to get things done. They apply these skills to fulfill their purpose and responsibility as leaders: serving others, volunteering, improving their community, and making a positive difference in the world around them.
>
> 2. Consider your own skill at getting things done. What past experiences have contributed to the development of this leadership skill in you? How have you been using sport to develop the ability to get things done in young people?
>
> 3. What new ideas about getting things done did this chapter awaken, and how can you apply these to facilitate youth leadership development in your sport setting?

Conclusion

All of the leadership skills mentioned in this book are learnable skills, not personality traits that only some people possess. When we awaken these skills in young people, we don't do so for that particular activity or context alone; we awaken these skills for life.

KEY TAKEAWAYS

1. *Leadership skills are for everyone.* They are not only for those who become team captains or stand out as potential leaders. Leadership skills can be learned by anyone and applied in any setting.
2. *Leadership skills should be developed in the same way that math or writing skills are developed.* This is the philosophy behind the CSDA phased model of leadership skills development. As a teacher would do in the

classroom with a new math concept, we first introduce or awaken leadership skills, then give young people a chance to practice those skills, and finally provide opportunities for application in authentic settings.

3. *Leadership skills can and should be applied throughout life in its various dimensions.* These skills are not just for the playing field or the workplace. We use communication, decision making, and other leadership skills in interactions with friends, family, and classmates; when planning a vacation or school project; when organizing a fund-raising event or a big surprise party. We want young people to leave our classrooms, programs, and sport settings and apply these leadership skills in all dimensions of their current and future lives.

4. *Leadership skills can be developed in many ways.* We use the sport platform because we have found it to be a powerful medium, but music and scouting are also powerful and authentic ways to develop leadership skills. We don't want to communicate that sport is the only way; it's just one way that has worked for us.

5. *Activity is only meaningful if young people are engaged.* Sometimes we have young people who just go through the motions; they're participating, but their minds are elsewhere. For the experiences to be meaningful and awaken leadership skills, young people must be engaged. After we set the experience in motion, we must observe. If the task is too easy, young people can

become distracted and disengaged; at that point, we must take action and modify the challenge as needed.
6. *Young people who apply these leadership skills can positively influence society in general.* Although we teach these skills in a sport setting, we want young people to carry them far beyond the field of play. We want them to become contributing members of society, those who use their leadership skills for the common good in their communities.

ACTIONS TO TAKE

1. *Reflect on what you've learned about leadership.* Take time to think about each of the skills and how they are or are not developed in your own life. Also reflect on the principles for developing these skills in others and ways you have or have not been doing so.
2. *Act on the knowledge that has been awakened.* That action might be in your direct engagement with young people in a sport setting, or it might be in sharing this information with others who work with youth through sports.
3. *Use this knowledge where relevant.* You may have read this book as a parent or volunteer at an after-school program. In such cases, you're not necessarily going to be designing learning experiences in a sport setting. However, if you have interactions with young people—your children, nieces, or nephews; your students or after-school participants; young people

in your neighborhood—you have opportunities to facilitate the development of leadership skills. You can still apply the philosophical ideas presented and approach young people with the awareness that they know things. They don't need to be told what to do; they need someone to come alongside and help them realize what they already know. If you're having a big family reunion, for example, instead of telling the children in the group to do something, ask them to organize part of the festivities. Let them brainstorm ideas, make a decision, use resourcefulness, and so on; then ask them about it later. That's a simple way of helping them develop leadership skills in authentic situations.

4. *Don't force this knowledge into spaces where it doesn't fit.* If the context of the community program does not involve a project with meaningful tasks that can be delegated, it's better to work on a different skill, not delegation. We want the delegated tasks to be authentic and real; we don't want young people feeling like we made something up to keep them busy. When we delegate, we are empowering people, making them feel valuable. Young people won't feel valued if we make up a task just so we can delegate. Likewise, if you have all the resources you need for a short-sided game, it's better to work on a different skill, not resourcefulness. We don't want to force young people to be creative and come up with a solution that really isn't

needed. In every situation, there are opportunities to facilitate one skill more appropriately than others. Sport will provide you with many opportunities for awakening knowledge in an authentic way; there's no reason to force it.

5. *As teachers, coaches, and facilitators, we have a responsibility to serve young people.* We sometimes label young people in a particular way based on our misunderstanding of who they are and what they really need. Don't write off any child like this. Don't label them as wayward or undisciplined or whatever based on what you see them doing or not doing. We have a responsibility to facilitate their development, no matter how they're acting. When we serve young people this way, we also model the way they should act toward others.

I wish you well in your efforts to develop the future leaders of the world.

Acknowledgments

My sincerest thanks to all the coaches, teachers, volunteers, and young people we've worked with over the years, who have helped awaken a better understanding and appreciation of how we can use sport as a tool for developing youth leaders.

+*ve vibes,*

Mark S. Mungal

About the Author

MARK MUNGAL is director and cofounder of the Caribbean Sport and Development Agency. Over the past two decades, he has facilitated workshops in thirteen English-speaking Caribbean territories and has spoken on youth leadership and sport at conferences from Switzerland to South Africa. Mark has been recognized as a thought leader in the arena of international sport for development, serving on several international, regional, and national agencies over the years. Mark continues to work with and learn from the dedicated coaches and volunteers who deliver sport programs in schools and communities and is committed to the development of Caribbean people through the amazing power of sport!

www.ingramcontent.com/pod-product-compliance
Lightning Source LLC
Chambersburg PA
CBHW032107090426
42743CB00007B/269